melvinna Atkins

THE CHEERLEADER'S GUIDE TO LIFE

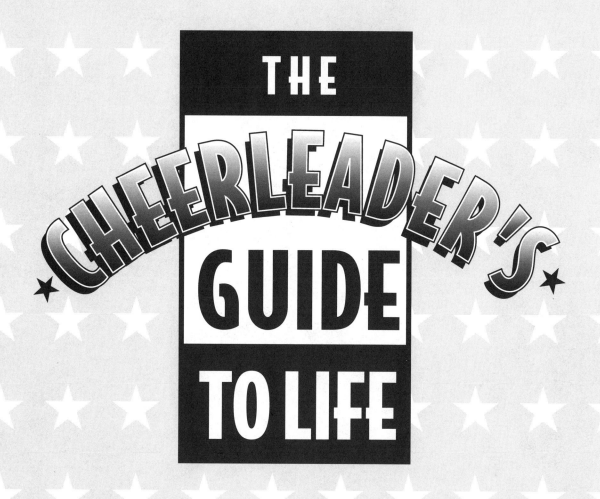

THE CHEERLEADER'S GUIDE TO LIFE

CINDY VILLARREAL

Harper*Perennial*
A Division of HarperCollins*Publishers*

HarperCollins books may be purchased for educational, business or sales promotional use. For information, please write: Special Markets Department, HarperCollins Publishers, Inc., 10 East 53rd Street, New York, NY 10022.

FIRST EDITION

Designed by Jessica Shatan

Library of Congress Cataloging-in-Publication Data
Villarreal, Cindy, 1965–
     The cheerleader's guide to life / by Cindy Villarreal.
         p.   cm.
     Includes index.
     ISBN 0–06–273291–9
     1. Cheerleading—United States.   I. Title.
LB3635.V55 1994
791.64—dc20   94–27910

94 95 96 97 ❖/CW 10 9 8 7 6 5 4 3 2 1

FOR MY HUSBAND ★ MASON HUGHES

This book is written in memory of my three cheerleader friends.
A portion of my royalties will benefit *For the Love of Christi*.

CONTENTS

CONTENTS

ACKNOWLEDGMENTS

My efforts in writing were made more productive through the cooperation and help of many people, whom I would like to thank now. Without their willingness to share their time and insights, this book would not have become what I believe is the most complete cheerleading book to date.

I would like to thank my agent, Jeff Herman, who was extremely helpful in getting the project in motion. Also, David Youngstrom and my editor, Rob Kaplan, both of whom saw the promise of the book and gave me the complete freedom to create and write the work on my own. Rob was great to work with and always took the time to help me with every detail. His assistant, Sandra Fox, was always extremely helpful. I would like to thank Joana Jebsen, Marilyn Spiegel and all those at the sales conference who made me feel so welcome. I would like to thank the production staff and art department for the book's cover and the book itself.

There are also many others behind the scenes who helped put the project together: My photographers who worked many long hours around my schedule to produce the works I requested—Margaret Kershaw, Geno Esponda and Mark Allred; and my illustrator Candice Eisenfeld, who was instrumental in making the crucial changes when needed and was very patient in doing so.

I thank my beautiful models—champion gymnast Kristie Phillips, Andrea Acosta, Leslie Ratley and Rhonda Gonzales. They were great sports during the tiring photo sessions. I also thank my model Tollie Bernard, whose strength was desperately needed to display the spotting procedures for partner stunts. My make-up artist Terry Jamail did a great job of keeping the models looking their best throughout the long, grueling hours. She always made sure the shoots went smoothly from start to finish. Rex Hawver and Art Elsasf of Crenshaw's Athletic Club of Austin made the photo shoots possible by providing the facilities. Debbie and Tony Leo of Pep Quarters and Jackie Rodgers and Richard Chadwick of Team Spirit made sure my models were properly uniformed by providing them with cheerleading uniforms and shoes.

Many friends in the industry were much more helpful than they realize, including Lucy Moore, Becky Rudolph and Ann Upchurch of K.A.P.O.S.; Susan True of the N.F.S.H.S.A. who put me in touch with K.A.P.O.S., among others; Angela King of U.S.A. Productions; Gwen Holtsclaw and David McAmis of Cheer Limited; Lawrence "Herkie" Herkimer, founder of the N.C.A.; Scott Elliott and the U.C.A. staff, who were so helpful in showing me around their wonderful camps; and a special thank you to the Kirby Jr. High School cheerleading squad of San Antonio, who were such a joy to visit at a time during the project when light was not yet visible at the end of the tunnel.

There were also many cheerleading and dance squad coaches, directors and trainers who took time out of their busy schedules to be interviewed. All played a key role in my capturing the cheerleading spirit. Among these I especially would like to thank Mary Barnes of the Los Angeles Raiderettes. Mary was more than willing to provide information that would help me help others get into cheerleading, and she was truly a joy to get to know. I am also grateful to Suzanne Mitchell, my Director when I was a Dallas Cowboys Cheerleader, for it is she who has sculpted much of my passion for this discipline. I also want to thank Raquel Navarez, Tamara Martin, the Philadelphia Eagles Cheerleaders and the Atlanta Falcons Cheerleaders for their wonderful photographs.

I thank Dr. Joseph A. Butts, M.D., Orthopedic Surgeon and Sports Medicine Specialist with the Institute of Sports Medicine in Richmond, Texas, who took time out of his extremely hectic schedule to provide pertinent safety and training information. His suggestions are valuable to anyone training for a cheerleading position. I also thank Jean Rubel of A.N.R.E.D., who was so helpful in providing me with nutritional and physiological information concerning eating disorders.

Thanks to Sandy Baker of Austin Writers League who answered my silliest questions and Jane Albritton for her helpful, enlightening words.

A heartfelt thanks to my lifelong friends the Speedy Gonzales family at Speedy's Printing in Austin for those last minute miracles they so graciously provided. Thanks to all my friends who encouraged me, including Chuck Meyer, Larry Bugan, Don and Susan Cox and everyone at their wonderful organization *For the Love of Christi*. And, finally, a special thanks to my family and friends for their love and encouragement.

INTRODUCTION

Ring...ring...ring. It was 11:45 P.M. Who could be calling at this hour? "Hello?" A voice on the other end introduced herself as a friend of an acquaintance of mine. Hot and tired from a Dallas Mavericks Dancers rehearsal, I did not feel like talking to anyone. "You don't know me," she began, "but I wanted to talk to you about becoming a cheerleader." I immediately knew why she was calling. I had received countless calls like this while cheerleading for the Dallas Cowboys Cheerleaders, but it was this particular phone call that prompted me to write this book. I immediately got to work and *The Cheerleader's Guide to Life* shifted into high gear.

As I began writing, I remembered how, as a first-timer on different squads, it was so difficult to figure out what to do first and what was most crucial for auditions. And it never failed, no matter how many questions I asked, there was still something else I needed to know that came up at the last minute. Not having a complete step-by-step guide to the many levels of preparation made it difficult for me to bring it all together at the right moment. I hope this book will help other future cheerleaders avoid that problem. Over the years I developed a simple, complete training system that proved very effective in gaining me squad positions against some of the stiffest competition around. I want to share with you my secrets of what it really takes to be a cheerleader at any level. I lead you here, each step of the way, by clarifying every detail so you'll never have to be as confused as I was.

This book is the culmination of my many years of experience in cheerleading, dance and instruction and virtually hundreds of interviews and consultations with cheerleaders, association representatives, squad directors, physicians and athletic trainers. It was fun to compile all the important details to help you become a cheerleader, but I never dreamed what an effort writing a book would be.

To some, cheerleading may seem an impossible dream, yet it is only the dreamer who can make dreams come true. For all the hopefuls—as I was—who dare to make cheerleading a reality, this book is for you. It is for the expert cheerleader who wants to earn a scholarship that will help pay the high cost of college tuition, for the pompon squad or mascot hopeful who wants to make a mark and for those who desire the fame and glamour of being on a professional squad.

This book is for all of you who have ever remotely thought of cheerleading, to guide you toward all the wonderful gifts cheerleading has to offer in life.

CINDY VILARREAL
Austin, Texas

★ PART I ★
YOUR WINNING SPIRIT

I believe having the right attitude is the source of superior performance, and ultimately determines how you view winning and losing. One of the most important aspects of cheerleading is your motivation. But sometimes motivating yourself to stretch beyond what you thought possible can become so mind-boggling it may seem easier to give up rather than try. But don't do this to yourself. The experiences you gain from attempting something difficult, like becoming a cheerleader, are perhaps more important than winning the spot itself. But before you undertake this great task, you have to focus your mind on achievement. Whether or not you ultimately wear a uniform you will be more fulfilled for having unleashed the cheerleader spirit within you.

★CHAPTER 1★

GO FOR THE GLORY

One-two-three-four, We want YOU to score six MORE!"

Wearing snow white bloomers, golden shirts with the letter C carefully stitched on the front and emerald and gold pompons we tirelessly fluffed then waved to the roaring crowd, our hearts soaring on wings of cheer. We were the Cook Cookie Cheerleaders whose fame reached the world over. Without a doubt we were the envy of every nine-year-old girl in the Universe!

We were proud of our team and determined to make a difference for them. I will never forget the pride that filled my soul before each game. We would overflow with giggles, laughter and anticipation. We greeted the fans with enthusiasm and electricity. We were a special group with a golden bond of friendship no other fourth-grade squad could equal. We were bitten by the bug early in life. And being in the uniform we had painstakingly designed produced a passion for more.

"They pulled it off," exclaimed one faculty member. We had had no actual faculty direction

or support, but we did it anyway. The school just hadn't realized the power of Cheer Fever.

Being in the limelight as a young cheerleader gave me the confidence and desire to reach for the stars throughout my life.

★ GO FOR THE GLORY: CHEER FEVER

Cheer Fever put magic into my childhood. I felt this very same fever as a rookie with the Dallas Cowboys Cheerleaders in front of 56,000 fans thirteen years later during the season's opening game against the Chicago Bears.

Cheer Fever was a driving force in my life. Nothing else had ever had such a profound influence. Once you've felt that spirit, it's as if there is nothing else. You are hooked.

This chapter will help you learn how to tap into your own driving force. Whether you are looking to cheer for your school or are ready for a professional career, it will take guts and goal-setting to go for the glory. You will need a carefully designed plan that will set you apart from every-

one else, because only a few are able to attain the coveted spots on any given squad.

Are you ready to build the foundation of your cheerleading dreams? Then keep on reading!

Lawrence "Herkie" Herkimer, founder of the National Cheerleader Association and inventor of the famous Herkie stunt jump, refers to catching the fever as a "taste of limelight."

Says Herkie, "Being out in front of the crowd and enticing them to cheer for the team is an experience most people never get: being on a football field, feeling the Astroturf under your feet, and being a part of the pomp and ceremony. Having the crowd respond to your commands gives you a big thrill when you get their response. Down on the sidelines where all the action is taking place, you have just as good a view of the game as the players, coaches and media. It's awesome to be down there in the magic of [thousands of] fans who would give their eye teeth to be down where you are."

No one enjoys the discipline required to do a

job well. But Cheer Fever is an exceptional reward. It can be a positive, powerful force in your life if you nourish it and harness its power.

Six Ways to Feed Cheer Fever

1. See how much of it you already have. If you enjoy being in the limelight you have the potential for a good case of Cheer Fever.

2. Take your temperature to see how much Cheer Fever you have. Ask yourself the following questions and rate your answers on a scale of one to ten, ten being the most.

- Do you enjoy being noticed by your friends?
- Do you enjoy speaking in public?
- Do you get excited when a group responds positively to your actions?
- Do you like performing?
- Do you like being told "that was great" and feeling like an expert?

Now, let's see how you did.

40–50 A definite case of cheer fever
25–39 You have the bug
10–24 A glimmer of hope
1–10 Are you alive?

If you scored twenty or above, you will find the following section has more power for you. But no matter what your score, the following steps will assist you in deciding whether cheerleading is right for you.

3. Harness the Fever. To take your enthusiasm and focus it toward your goal, you can do the following exercise:

Get a notepad and pencil, and then brainstorm. Visualize yourself cheerleading on the field. Write down a description of the picture you see. Examine that mental picture of yourself. What is different about the you in your visualization than the you in real life?

- Do you appear to be more confident?
- Are you more attractive and better groomed?
- How good are your cheerleading skills?
- What organization or squad did you belong to?
- Are you happy with a positive attitude?

Okay, now ask yourself if you like what you see in the image you have created. Now make a list of the things that differ from the image you visualized and reality. Then develop a strategy to bring yourself to that level of excellence.

- Can you improve your appearance?
- Do you need to learn more mechanical skills?
- Do you believe in yourself?

Think carefully as you write each one down. Learn to harness your potential by visualizing your goals and aspirations. The difference between what you dream about and what you can achieve is the will to try. Your dreams *can* become reality. The mind is our most powerful tool. If you visualize something, the mind sets about trying to figure a solution to the problem you have presented. It is much like a computer. Stay focused on your dream and you will find ways to achieve your goals. It takes a deep desire and commitment to make things happen. If you expect great things you will achieve them.

4. Take action. Visualizing gives the mind the ability to seek solutions to problems. However, it is up to you to take action with your own creative ideas. Even though cheerleading is a team event, when you are trying out you are going to be judged on you alone. Your inner voice will reliably lead you to success.

One exercise is to list your cheerleading goals and list five ways to accomplish each one, in order of priority.

5. Objectively examine strengths and weaknesses. Realistically examine whatever might hinder you from reaching your desired cheerleading goals:

- Do you get stage fright?
- Are you so afraid of failing you would rather not try
- Do you have bad grades?
- Do you tend to have a negative attitude?
- Do you have two left feet and otherwise weak skills?

Now write down any obstacles you might face. Go item by item and determine if the problem can realistically be changed.

If you have an obstacle that can't be changed, don't be discouraged. Even if you don't try out for the cheerleading squad there are many ways you can be involved with your team that are fun and satisfying. We will discuss them in later chapters.

If your obstacles are caused by fears, you must work very hard to overcome them.

6. Extinguish the fire that feeds your fears. Like most fires, this one spreads wildly. It burns and destroys any wish you may have for self-achievement. How often do you tell yourself, "I'm not sure I can do it. I'm afraid"? Other fears you may experience might be like the following:

- "What will my friends say if I fail?"
- "I never succeed at anything. Maybe I should give up."
- "She always gets everything. It's not fair."
- "If I stop trying now, maybe I can stop embarrassing myself."
- "Everyone likes her better than me. No one will notice me."

Nonsense! You can do it! What if I had listened to my own fears when our elementary school teachers said that we could not succeed in forming the Cook Cookie Cheerleaders on our own? If I had listened to those fears when I tried out for the Dallas Cowboys Cheerleaders, I would have let fear defeat me. None of my friends expected me to make it, saying, "Nobody ever makes it the first time to try out." The easy way out would have been to not try at all.

But those joys I experienced would have been lost to a fearful, defeated attitude that would have affected me the rest of my life. Because I took action, I conquered my fears to bring my goals to life. Practice harnessing the fever to take action toward your desired goal. *Remember, action conquers fear.*

★ A STATE OF MIND

Your attitude influences the "mind." Imagine it like this: Your attitude is a pair of glasses that colors images of everything you experience. A positive attitude will paint successful images in your mind. It finds good things and reminds you that you deserve a pat on the back for your successes. This attitude builds your confidence because your experiences make you feel successful. You will try more challenging tasks with the belief that you will succeed. You *will* try, and you *will* succeed. You aren't just born with self-confidence and perseverance. People who work on these traits typically enjoy a successful outcome. *Your actions toward your fears determine how much self-esteem you have. When you take action against your inner fears you will build self-esteem.*

Three Key Attitude Enhancers

1. Confidence Believe in yourself. Expect the best. Set realistic goals, avoiding comparisons with others. Take action in completing a step toward your desired goal. You will feel confidence when you overcome just one step toward a goal. Actions toward goals build confidence.

2. Motivation Your degree of desire for a positive outcome is a measure of your motivation. Remember the mental image of yourself as you would like to be? That mental picture is your incentive. Do you want to change yourself into that image? We don't have to stay the way we are if we do not want to. You have nothing to lose. Step out on that limb and take a chance—you will be better off than if you had never tried at all.

A much worse feeling is the "What if Syndrome." The "What if Syndrome" plants negative seeds and confirms your fears. It is knowing you might have succeeded had you tried, but you passed up a one-time opportunity for fear of failure.

"What if I had tried out for the squad? I was better than Janet." You will have only this memory to look back on, but Janet will have all the memories of having been on the squad. Even if you come up short, trying always feels better than the regret of not knowing.

3. Commitment It's great that you're motivated right now. But for how long? The trick is to keep taking actions and steps toward accomplishing your goals even when you feel it's hopeless. Just remember, ability is only a small part of success. Sticking to the task is what counts.

More people fail because of lack of commitment than for any other reason. Not only is commitment the most important thing when training, it's also the most subject to attack by your failures along the way. Failures are just as important as triumphs because they often offer the most important lessons. So stop calling them failures and refer to them as learning experiences.

★ MY STORY

I Went for the Glory

I was a scared and insecure fourteen-year-old freshman forced into an alien environment called High School. It was a sweltering late August day in Austin, Texas, and practicing my routines was a self-inflicted torture that tested my commitment daily.

I Visualized My Dream Position

I desperately wanted to be like my sister who was popular in high school. Even I knew her popularity took off when she tried out for the high-school dance team four years earlier. So I practiced as hard as I could, even though I thought it might kill me.

Fear Attacked My Commitment

Although I had dance training since age four, there were many upperclassmen trying out who were all better than me. When I thought of get-

ting "cut" my heart would sink. I knew that not trying out would be much easier. To audition for the dance team, I had to exhibit skill and expertise in front of everybody. My older sister had just graduated from high school, was one of the original National Champions and one of the few freshmen who made the team her first time out. I felt pressured and I was afraid. I had always compared myself to her, and deep inside I thought my parents did too. My pride painted a different portrait than reality. I didn't want other people to see the stress this was causing in me. My stomach felt queasy at the thought of having to tell anyone if I didn't make it. I might have to disguise myself for the rest of the year and change my name to Jones. I wouldn't even bother to tell my sister it would just confirm her suspicion that I was a dweeb.

I Harnessed Cheer Fever to Help Drive My Actions

Being a part of that National Championship dance team was one of my biggest aspirations. Known for being skilled performers, the girls were very popular, well conditioned and beautiful. If I made it, it would be my ticket to instant popularity. In fact, performing with that elite, wonderful group would be one of the highlights of my life.

My Actions Conquered My Fears

For six months I practiced several hours a day, memorizing steps and style positions. Using the constructive criticism from others, my high kicks got higher, my splits flattened and my confidence grew stronger.

One hundred and forty-seven girls tried out that rainy February morning, with only eighteen spots open for freshmen. There were many tears shed before tryouts because the odds of our making it were slim. With each routine, I practiced showmanship and confidence. As I turned to wish my friends good luck, I overheard a girl say, "Oh, she'll make it because her sister was one." That remark hurt. I took a deep breath, a moment in prayer, and reminded myself that no one had done all that hard work for me. If I would be selected, it would be because I earned it.

I went for the glory. Even if I didn't make it there would be no "What if Syndrome" for me.

I knew those months of practice had paid off when they called my name and number. Yes, I made it!

★ WHAT SPARKS CHEER FEVER?

Whether it's America's love of sports, the desire to root and yell for your favorite team or the instant popularity, immediate respect and recognition you receive from being a cheerleader, Cheer Fever provides hope, promise and perseverance both on and off the field. "Cheerleaders make high-energy professionals," says Herkie. Cheerleaders have a certain spirit that causes their creativity and enthusiasm to carry over into life.

★CHAPTER 2★

WHAT DOES IT TAKE?

Do you have the fever? Yes? Now what does it take for you to become part of the cheerleading legacy? There is much more to cheerleading than looking cute, jumping around and shaking your pompons.

"Cheerleading is extremely athletic," says Katie Demory, Assistant Director of Student Activities at North Dakota State University. "I used to think the cheerleaders just wanted to meet the players and were there to be pretty. Now I know it's much more sophisticated than that."

Cheerleading requires much training and preparation. You need to be willing to get sweat in your eyes, a sore throat from yelling and frequent aching muscles. It takes eating right, plenty of exercise and adequate rest. Cheerleading means hard work, dedication and the courage to try even when it looks as if all the odds are against you. You'll be held to a higher standard of excellence in many of the things that you do, and will be expected to set a good example for your peers.

If you are looking for fun you will not be disappointed. But do not think for a minute that you can glide through the experience on your good looks. If you improve your skills and basic mechanics, your tryout experience will be much more enjoyable.

★ GROWING PAINS

Leah, an eighth grader from Indianapolis, Indiana, learned this lesson the hard way. She discovered that popularity is not nearly as important as preparation. Trying out for cheerleader is like interviewing for a job. Employers will always hire the person they feel has the best skills and a willingness to learn more. While attractiveness and charm may be a consideration, making it the basis for a decision could have embarrassing consequences.

Leah explains:

I tried all year to be nice to everyone so I could make the cheerleading squad. They even

elected me class favorite, so I felt great about my chances. I saw all the other girls practicing, but rationalized, "Who knew them?" I had more friends than everyone. I kept thinking, "How hard could it be to try out and make it?"

During the week of tryouts we learned the group yells. When they showed us the jumps, I knew I was in trouble. After school I called a former cheerleader to ask for some help. Her mom said she was busy with homework and would not get back to me until morning. The trouble was, tryouts were the next day and that was too late. I was panicking. When I got to the gym, I took a good look at my competition and I realized how unprepared I was. I really didn't think jumps would be that important, but I'll know next time.

Leah did not make the squad but was able to turn her bad situation into a learning opportunity. I hear stories like hers often. Contrary to popular belief, there is no perfect mold; you don't have to be the most popular, a part-time model or beauty pageant winner to become a cheerleader. Leah failed because she compared her popularity to others' instead of improving her abilities. Leah waited until the last moment to prepare because she thought mechanics wouldn't matter. It kept her from achieving her full potential.

Cheerleading is a team activity. No individual is more privileged or more important. What Leah learned was that she would have to work as hard as everyone else for what she wanted. Preparation is the key—it separates those who make it the first time from those who must try out again.

"I lost to myself," remarks Leah.

★ THE SELF-DEFEATING SYNDROME

The "Self-Defeating Syndrome" is a pattern of behavior that directly or indirectly contributes to your failure to achieve your goals. In other words, you cause yourself to blow it because of things you definitely could change. Examples are:

1. Procrastination. Procrastination is when you put something off until the last minute: "Oh, just one more television show and then I'll practice," or "Tryouts aren't for another two weeks."

If you have ever had to cram or work extra hard because you frittered away your time, you are well on the road to understanding the art of procrastination. As you learned from Leah, it is much easier to learn something like a jump with a little practice every day than trying to do it all at once. And don't forget, if you make the squad you will need to keep up with your studies because you will not have the time to procrastinate. So make this a rule: Aspiring cheerleaders do not procrastinate.

2. Lack of confidence. If you do not believe that you are "good enough" to be a cheerleader, you are going to greatly reduce your chances of making the squad. People tend to reflect what they believe about themselves. For example, it is not uncommon for people to walk out of a tryout because they have psyched themselves out so badly that they think they would be better off not trying at all. Or they allow their negative thinking to make them too nervous to perform to their maximum ability.

There is no instant cure for a lack of confidence. It is helpful to read what are called affirmations. You can easily make a 3" x 5" card of positive affirmations. Affirmations are sentences that "affirm" or reinforce what it is you wish to believe. Read or say these sentences over and over whenever you feel nervous or underconfident. They really do help. They undo all the negative sentences you say to yourself, replacing them with healthier thoughts.

Some examples that may be helpful for you are:

- I can do anything if I believe in myself.
- I am talented.
- I am beautiful inside and out.
- I can learn anything if I try.
- There is a wonderful cheerleader spirit in me.
- I will remain calm and relaxed.

These sentences can be changed according to the negative thought you are trying to counteract. The trick is being aware of the self-defeating messages you might be giving to yourself every day.

3. Overconfidence. This might also be referred to as conceit. No matter what you call it, it can be deadly to your chances. If you are overconfident like our friend Leah, you are not going to put in the hard work you need to make the squad. You are also going to be like the hare, not the tortoise. If you snooze, you will lose. Some "less special" girl is going to sneak up behind you and grab your spot. Cheerleading is not a one-girl showcase. There are no stars. If you behave like a soloist you will most likely be cut. If you are not cut, the others, including the coaches, might wish that you were.

How will I know if I'm overconfident? If you are asking this question, there is hope for you. Just be aware of your attitude and never dwell on being better than other people. Use yourself as your only gauge of competition.

4. Poor attention to details. "I'm sorry, coach, I thought tryouts were tomorrow." Certainly missing appointments, practices and tryouts is not going to help your chances. However, there are other details to which you need to pay attention. If your coach says stand in a certain place, stand there. If the coach says fill out a certain form, fill it out and return it on time. Cheerleading is a precision activity. If you are going to be chronically late or "scatterbrained," you could be a detriment to the rest of the squad. Whatever you do during tryouts will be used to determine what kind of teammate you will be.

Learning to pay attention to details is not easy if it is not natural to you—but it can be done. You need to focus on the tasks and set up systems to make sure you don't forget. Many people have trouble with organization which is why so many companies make a lot of money selling things like trapper keepers, folders and appointment notebooks. You should pick up any number of these things to help you get control over the details in your life.

Do not throw notices in your backpack or rely on memory. Make it easier for yourself by taking a few extra minutes to write things down, organize and file them. Wouldn't it be silly to miss out on a spot on a team because your dog ate your notice about cheerleading tryouts?

Other ways to avoid self defeat:

1. Preparation. Get ready by starting early. Be persistent in planning your actions. Step-by-step, follow the path this book provides. The fact that you are reading this book shows that you care and gives you an advantage.

2. Inquire. Ask the sponsor or coach questions and learn as much as you can before tryouts. No matter how much you think you know, there are still many things to learn.

3. Attitude. Balance your confidence level and focus on self-development. Remember, proper preparation with a good attitude is a powerful package.

★MIND OVER MATTER

You really can overcome obstacles with a good attitude. Current cheerleader Andrea Acosta, now in her early twenties, shares her triumphant story of how she was able to overcome adversity by not giving in to self-defeat.

One day in the seventh grade I heard the students talking about who would try out for cheerleader. "I'd like to try out," I proudly announced. "You can't be a cheerleader," one girl snipped at me, "because you can't even see the chalkboard from the front row!" True, I could not see the chalkboard, however, I'd feel completely useless if I let my visual impairment get the best of me. I suffered a maternity ward accident as an infant that caused me to be legally blind in my left eye, with only light perception in my right. At the age of four I had cataract surgery and was diagnosed with glaucoma. I've faced tremendous obstacles in the past and her dismal remark was just the motivation I needed. I am one to stand up for myself, and cheerleading was my benchmark.

Andrea believed in herself, worked extra hard and made the squad. The other girl didn't. Like Leah, the other girl was more focused on the other girls weaknesses than on developing her own strengths.

Most people would assume that Andrea wasn't capable of becoming a cheerleader because she was visually impaired. Determined to make up for her vision, Andrea harnessed her desire to become a cheerleader and worked methodically against the odds. Today she is among the best cheerleaders I have ever witnessed in action.

From her early days in junior high, she was selected All-American Cheerleader. She was a cheerleader for the University of Texas for an unprecedented three years, and is currently a staff instructor with the National Cheerleading Association.

★PERSISTENCE PAYS OFF

Some people seem born with persistence but others have to reach for it. If you think about how much you want to reach your goal, you can develop the drive it will take to get there. You are the only one who can do this for you. There is no substitute for persistence.

Try this self-assessment and see how you do. No one is going to see your grade except you, so be brutally honest. The purpose of the assessment is to recognize your strengths and learn ways to overcome your personal weaknesses. Rate yourself on a scale of 1 to 5, one being "poor," two "fair", three "average", four "good" and five "excellent."

Self-Assessment

1. Confidence. Do you believe you have what it takes to accomplish your goals?

1   2   3   4   5

2. Leadership. Do your peers look to you as an example for problem solving and personal direction?

1   2   3   4   5

3. Considerate. Are you courteous with other people, and do you show respect?

1   2   3   4   5

4. Responsible. Can you be counted on to be on time and follow through with commitments?

1   2   3   4   5

5. Integrity. Are you honest and truthful?

1   2   3   4   5

6. Cooperative. Can you share and work in a team setting?

1   2   3   4   5

7. Determination. Are willing to work extra hard, in order to accomplish the goals of the squad?

1   2   3   4   5

8. Optimistic. Do you look for the positive in every situation?

1   2   3   4   5

9. Discipline. Are you able to control your behavior and give or take constructive criticism to achieve a favorable outcome?

1   2   3   4   5

10. Enthusiastic. Are you a good sport, and do you encourage team spirit and group involvement?

1   2   3   4   5

How Can I Tell If I Have It?

If you are still reading, you are on the right track. Always be in a position to learn. Cheerleaders, even the most experienced ones, are continually improving their skills, expanding their knowledge and developing ways to better their team program. Cheerleading requires preparation, leadership, athleticism and good sportsmanship. These qualities take time to nourish, and we all possess each of them to different degrees. With a little conscious effort to develop these traits and a willingness to work hard to obtain the basics, you can build a bridge to your dream and maybe even beyond.

As a quick summary, let's review some of the main aspects of this chapter. Making the cheerleading squad and being a highly successful cheerleader is about having the basic ABCs.

★ THE CHEERLEADER'S ABCS

A is for Attitude, **B** is for Benevolence, **C** is for Confidence, **D** is for Dependability, **E** is for Enthusiasm, **F** is for Fitness, **G** is for Grooming, **H** is for Honesty, **I** is for Integrity, **J** is for Jumps, **K** is for Knowledge, **L** is for Leadership, **M** is for Motivation, **N** is for Nutrition, **O** is for Optimism, **P** is for Practice, **Q** is for Questions, **R** is for Rest, **S** is for Spirit, **T** is for Tenaciousness, **U** is for Unity, **V** is for Victoriousness, **W** is for Will, **X** is for eXtra perfect stunts, **Y** is for Yells, and last, but certainly not least, **Z** is for Zeal!

Read them again and again. Beginning with the next chapter, we will get started with some solid basics!

★ PART II ★
LET'S CHEER!

Cheerleading began because sports are such an important part of our American Culture. Spirit is at the heart of sports, and sports are at the heart of cheerleading.

If you want to be a cheerleader, it is going to be important for you to know the history of cheerleading and the rules of the game. I recall how embarrassed I was in junior high school when I cheered loudly for our opponent after they took *our* ball away.

Another junior high cheerleader I knew was asked by a fan, "Who just made that touchdown?" To which she replied, "What touchdown?"

As you've already learned, we are more than just pretty faces. So be sure to learn where we as cheerleaders have come from, where we are going, and what the position calls us to do.

★CHAPTER 3★

HISTORY OF CHEERLEADING

t all began during a Princeton University football game in the early 1880s when the first recorded yell

Ray, Ray, Ray!
Tiger, Tiger, Tiger!
Sis, Sis, Sis!
Boom, Boom, Boom!
Aaaaaaah! Princeton, Princeton, Princeton!

was performed in locomotion style. It wasn't hip hop, but it was very catchy, and it started a phenomena. You have to remember, this was the time of bustles, high-topped shoes and few forms of group entertainment. Cheering struck a chord with spectators who loved getting directly involved with the excitement on the field.

In 1884 Thomas Peebles, a graduate of Princeton, carried the yell to the University of Minnesota campus. It was there that cheer "leading" made its true mark (as we know it today). One of the cheerleaders, Johnny Campbell, got

so excited that he couldn't resist jumping out in front of the crowd.

He took the initiative and suggested the election of six men, to lead a yell on the sidelines before the student body. (There were no female cheerleaders back then.) When they introduced the squad the crowd followed in roaring unison. *The Ariel*, the university's student news publication, documented the event in a story that appeared in the November 12, 1898, issue. The story, as it appeared in *The Ariel*, states "If organization and yelling and pageantry can do it [help the team win] the result we desire will be accomplished. Yelling captains have been elected to take charge of the rooting and conduct it in a systematic and effective manner."[1]

The newspaper further promoted the yell captains and listed these, your predecessors:

The following men were nominated to lead the yelling today: Jack Campbell, F. G. Kotlaba, M. J. Luby, Albert Armstrong of the Academics, Wickersham of the Laws,

Litzenburg of the Medics. These men should see to it that everybody leaves the park today breathless and voiceless—as this is the last game here, it ought to be a revelation to the people of Minnesota in regard to University enthusiasm.[2]

To them, breathless and voiceless was a new phenomenon. Today it is an expectation.

Unsatisfied with sitting in the grandstand watching the guys on the gridiron give their blood and risk broken noses for a victory, those first cheerleaders wanted a front seat, so they could savor every action of the game.

Those enthusiastic supporters of their alma mater could not possibly fathom that the enthusiasm they unveiled to the city of Minneapolis was a new kind of spirit leading, destined for high-profile recognition. From this point forward, spirit yelling would be in the forefront of sports, "cheer" leading the way.

Those inventive founding fathers of cheerleading are a tough act to follow. They were chosen for their personal character and integrity in addition to their performing charisma. They became involved in the community and ultimately became the business and political leaders of our society.

In the 1920s the yell leaders brought in beating drums and noise makers to add variety to their performances. As the popularity of American football developed, cheerleading became more popular than ever.

The next major change in the style and execution of cheerleading was during the early 1940s. As with many vocations, World War II changed cheerleading from long pants to long skirts. Men went off to war, and women stepped into factory work, baseball uniforms and onto cheerleading squads. As our men were off defending Europe and Asia, women continued to work hard at home, revitalizing the tradition of spirit at a time when national spirit was badly needed.

Since women were here to stay after the boys returned from war, cheerleading could incorporate some new twists and turns. The teams added partner stunts and gymnastics to the sidelines.

There was a definite division of labor. The males *always* did the gymnastics, and only the girls danced. This division of labor gave rise to collegiate drill and dance squads.

In 1948 the San Francisco 49ers added a majorette "baton twirling dance" squad to their professional team. Of course, today more and more girls learn gymnastics, and it's chic for boys to dance too.

At this time, cheerleading was becoming more sophisticated and needed more organization. Lawrence "Herkie" Herkimer, who had received notoriety in gymnastics and cheerleading, decided to teach the art of precision cheerleading at summer camps. He founded the first cheerleading organization, the National Cheerleading Association (NCA), in 1948. Not long after, other cheerleading associations started up.

Herkie created spirit slogan ribbons and booster buttons as a way to help cheerleaders raise money to come to camps. These methods are still used today.

The 1960s ushered in perhaps the most important invention in cheerleader history, pompons. Most people now can hardly visualize a cheerleader without one.

The NCA initiated the trend using paper pompons. When they discovered that colorful paper pompons and rain did not mix, they were replaced by vinyl.

Smaller "show poms" are the vogue now because of all the dancing the cheerleaders do. Large pompons are still preferred for large stadium audiences. And the smaller pompons are preferred for closer audiences.

The 1960s were wonderful years for cheerleading since the popularity of professional sports was growing. The Baltimore [now Indianapolis] Colts led the way for cheerleaders to join the professional ranks with the first professional cheerleading squad in history. Until then the few teams that had squads relied upon high school cheerleaders to double for the pro teams. These squads only performed precision sideline cheers.

In 1972 Tex Schramm, General Manager for the Dallas Cowboys, challenged Texie Waterman, a former Broadway dancer, to create something new with professionals. No more sideline cheers, just pure pompon "Broadway-style" jazz dance entertainment for the sidelines. This departure from traditional cheerleading brought with it some major changes to professional teams.

In 1976, at Super Bowl X, a television camera captured one cheerleader's "All-American" wink. So many people responded that the phenomenon sent the Dallas Cowboys Cheerleaders on to international stardom. Soon virtually every professional team created its own team of talented ladies and sent them onto their courts and sidelines to entertain. It's what the public wanted.

The success was incredible. Unlike cheerleading as we knew it, the latest evolution of "dancing" cheerleaders was born. Big crowds, world travel, TV appearances and media hype meant the girls were polished in every way possible. Today, the Los Angeles Rams cheerleaders are the only professional cheerleading squad performing advanced, elite stunts in a traditional cheerleading fashion.

There were other important and positive changes for cheerleaders in the 1970s. The passage of Title IX in 1972 provided equal athletic opportunities for women. The increased athletic participation by women furthered the need for cheerleader attendance at both men's and women's sporting events. Scholarships soon became available to women athletes and cheerleaders. The late 1970s also saw the beginning of regular high school and collegiate cheerleading competitions.

After the first one hundred years of cheerleading history, the late 1980s provided high school cheerleaders with universal standards they could follow. Now recognized as a true athletic form, the cheerleader safety guidelines outlawed many dangerous tumbling moves, pyramids over two levels high, and the mini-trampoline after several students were tragically injured.

The 1990s offer interesting challenges as more and more males take a bigger interest in traditional cheerleading. There's also good news for university students; collegiate pom and dance squads are now the fastest growing segment in the spirit leading industry. Cheerleading is at a new all-time high, having captured the attention of Japan, Europe, Canada and Mexico. And some professional teams have even brought aboard junior cheerleaders for occasional performing.

You can see that the history of cheerleading has been an important part of our nation's history. Cheerleading was born because some special people did not want to spend their lives sitting in the grandstand watching life pass them by.

Some very interesting people have been cheerleaders in years past: Two cheerleaders became Presidents of the United States: Dwight D. Eisenhower[3] and Ronald Reagan.[4]

Some others include: Susan Lucci, Phyllis George, Katie Couric and Paula Abdul.

The future of cheerleading is in the hands of people like you. It will be an exciting journey to your own winning traditions as you carry the torch to victory.

[1] "Everybody yell!" *Ariel* XXII (1898): 129.

[2] "The Northwestern game today." *Ariel* XXII (1898): 127.

[3] Westpoint Yearbook, 1915.

[4] Ronald Reagan, *An American Life* (New York: Simon & Schuster, 1990).

★CHAPTER 4★

SPORTS AND TEAM HISTORY

For some of you, cheerleading would be fun with or without any association with a team. Many girls wouldn't know a line of scrimmage from a goal post. Just remember that cheerleading exists only because it enhances the experience of spectator sports. Therefore it is really important that you learn sports basics so you will be able to fully participate during the game. Before I became interested in cheerleading, the only thing I knew about sports was that whoever had the most points won the game. Sports games can be rather confusing if you don't at least understand what the rules are and how a team earns points. Gaining basic knowledge of the games is the easiest aspect of preparing for tryouts, but it is also the one most often overlooked. It is important for a cheerleader to know what to cheer for and when cheering is appropriate during the game, so don't get caught without this simple knowledge.

Cheerleading requires a variety of sports knowledge. You can spare yourself many embar-rassing situations in front of the judges and stu-dent body by taking ten minutes to brush up on a few facts. Your coach may want you to be familiar with other particular facts of your school teams. But even if it is not required, you may have an opportunity to work some of it in during your interview. Try to familiarize yourself with the fol-lowing school and team facts:

1. When was your school founded and for whom is it named?

2. What are your team's colors?

3. What is the story behind the selection of the mascot?

4. What is your school's hand sign if any?

5. Do you know the history behind your school fight song and school song?

6. Can you recite your school motto and creed?

You can find the answers to these questions by visiting your school's administration office, the school library and yearbook department. Learning why your school has certain traditions will be fun and very interesting.

Cheerleaders are ambassadors of goodwill for their schools. Your increased understanding of your school's history and traditions will heighten your experience as a student and can only be a bonus for your consideration as a member of the squad. It will help you gain school spirit which will certainly shine through.

Here are basic facts to get you started with the various games. If you need more, your school library should have some useful material.

Sports Officials

Officials are responsible for supervising a game according to the proper rules. They should be treated with respect even if you don't agree with their decisions because, aside from it being good manners, it could have bad repercussions for your team. The officials call both offensive and defensive penalties. Although fans and some squads cheer when the penalty is against the opposing team, it is improper and unsportsmanlike to cheer when a penalty is called.

★FOOTBALL

The object of football is to score the most touchdowns. The game begins with a **kickoff.** The receiving team returns the ball as far as possible until the runner is tackled by someone on the kicking team.

Each play in football is called a **down.** The team with the ball (**offense**) has four downs to make at least ten yards (a **first down**). For each first down, the offense is given another four downs. That sequence is repeated until an offensive player crosses the **goal line** with the ball (**touchdown**).

7. What traditions are unique to your school?

8. Has your school won any sports championships?

9. How has your school's "homecoming" changed through the years?

10. Who founded your school's first pep or spirit organization?

11. What year were your school's first cheerleading squad and pep organizations added?

12. How many cheerleading squads does your school have?

13. What division does your team play in?

14. What sports and activities does the squad participate in?

15. What distinguished awards has your school received?

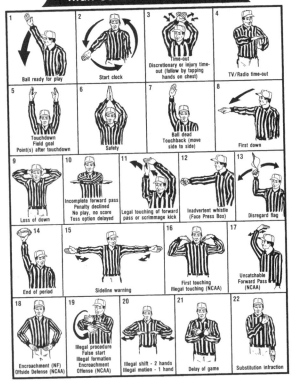

NOTE: Signals number 25 and 26 are for future expansion.

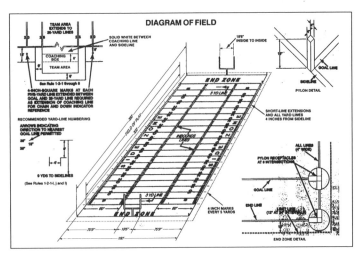

The team trying to stop the offense is the **defense.** If the offense fails to make at least ten yards during any of the four down opportunities, it must give the ball up to the defensive team so they get their offensive turn. Most teams give up the ball on fourth down by **punting** or if they are close enough to the desired goal line, they may attempt a **field goal** for three points.

The officials crew includes a referee, a lines-

man, an umpire and one or more judges. The referee, wearing the white cap, has the most responsibility. The above are reference drawings for hand signals and their meaning. It is good to familiarize yourself with them because it will help you follow the game. After each hand signal the referee will point to indicate who was penalized. Sometimes both teams will commit penalties during the same play and the referee will make a judgment on what to do after he has made all hand motions and indicated each team. These are called offsetting penalties.

DEFINITIONS

Offense The team with the ball.

Defense The team that is trying to take the ball from the offense while defending its own goal line.

Touchdown A player takes the ball over the opposing team's goal line. It is worth six points.

Point after Touchdown A ball kicked through the uprights of the goal post on the play after a touchdown; sometimes called the "extra point." It is worth one point.

Field Goal A ball kicked through the uprights of the goal post, except on a kickoff or the play following a touchdown. It is worth three points.

Goal Line The zero yard line at each end of the football field.

Pass A ball thrown by a member of the offensive team, usually the quarterback, to a qualified teammate.

Interception A pass caught by a member of the defensive team.

First Down An award of four new downs to an offensive team for gaining ten or more yards within four downs.

Punt Most advantageous method for the offensive team to give the defensive team the ball; usually on fourth down with a special, long center snap to the kicker.

Line of scrimmage The imaginary line across the field where the ball is placed before a play begins.

Kickoff The kicking team kicks the ball to the receiving team to begin a new half of play, or after the kicking team has scored a touchdown or a field goal.

★BASKETBALL

Another popular game is basketball. Basketball is played with five players on each team. The game starts with a **jump ball** in the center circle. One member of each team tries to tip the ball to a teammate. Each team consists of five players including a captain. The team who wins the jump (**offense**) will have **24 seconds** to attempt a scoring shot. If the shot scores, the ball automatically turns over to the other team, and they have 24 seconds to attempt a shot. The 24-second shot clock resets and starts over if the shot is unsuccessful and the **rebound** is recovered by the team who made the failed shot attempt. If the defending team gets the rebound or turnover they are constrained by the shot clock. This sequence repeats itself, interrupted by many penalties and much excitement until game time expires.

College basketball is officiated by one referee and one umpire. Each official has special duties to administer during the game. The referee shoulders more responsibilities officiating the game procedures. The umpire and the referee share responsibilities in officiating player rules of conduct and penalties.

Official Basketball Signals

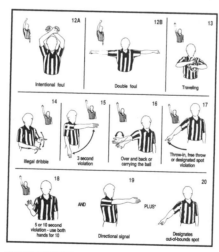

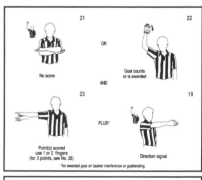

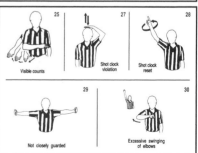

The numbers assigned to each signal correspond with the numbering in the Collegiate Commissioners Association officiating manuals.

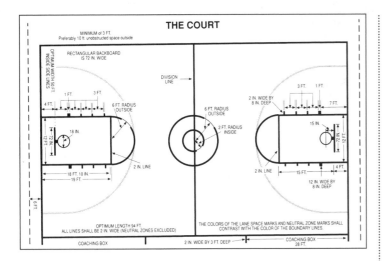

THE COURT

DEFINITIONS

Offense The team with the ball.

Defense The team trying to take the ball from the offense.

Jump Ball Used to start a game or put the ball in play after a dead ball has been declared. This is done by standing off two opposing players in the center circle of the court and the official tosses the ball straight up between them for each to try to gain possession.

Dead Ball A ball that is declared out of play by an official.

Twenty-four Second Clock Begins when a team gains possession of the ball to assure that the team attempts a scoring shot before the clock has reached 24 seconds.

Field Goal When a player throws the ball into the basket. It's worth two or three points depending on the distance from which it is thrown.

Free Throw A free shot from the free throw line awarded to a player who has been fouled. One point.

Throw In A method to put the ball in play after it has been declared dead. The ball is often turned over to the defensive team in this manner.

Rebound The live ball that bounces away from the backboard after it misses the basket.

Technical Foul A penalty charged, usually to an entire team, for illegal game strategy (except for individual gross misconduct). On the third

infraction by a team the coach may be ejected from the game.

Personal Foul A penalty called on an individual player for improper play. A player is allowed five personal fouls before ejection from the game.

★ICE HOCKEY

Ice Hockey is played on an ice surface called a rink. Each team consists of six players wearing skates and equipped with protective gear and a curved stick to hit the puck into the opponents goal. The game begins with a **face off** between two opposing players in the center ring. The team who gains possession of the puck strategically passes back and forth between teammates while trying to hit it into the goal. The defending team tries to take the puck away from the attacking team. If they are successful in intercepting the puck, they become the attacking team. A face off at the center of the ring follows a successfully completed goal. This exciting sequence of plays and penalties repeats until the game time has expired but not without the interruption of many penalties and much excitement.

Two linesmen and one referee officiate in ice hockey. The referee has full jurisdiction of the game and his decisions are final. The referee is responsible for supervising the events of the game and imposing penalties. Team penalties may be called against both offensive and defensive teams. Depending on the penalty, it is common for players to be in the penalty box (out of the game) for extended periods.

DEFINITIONS

Face off The dropping of the game puck between two opposing players to begin the game or to put the puck back into play after it is blown dead.

Playmaker The player who sets up the plays and gives signals.

Pass When one player hits the puck to another on the same team.

Goalie The defending player who stands in front of the goal net at each end of the ring. He wears the most body padding and defends the goal against incoming offensive puck shots.

Foul Any penalty.

Attack An aggressive offensive effort to make a goal.

Penalty box The area where players remain while being penalized.

Save A goalie blocking a shot.

Goal A shot which makes it into the net. It is worth one point.

★WRESTLING

A wrestling match is an event between two athletes in a similar weight class and is held on a padded surface called a mat. A match consists of two very short periods or bouts. The wrestlers are judged on technical superiority against their opponent and are awarded points for holds, moves and pinning their opponent to the mat.

Wrestling is both an individual and a team sport. Each member of the team has his own match, but all points accumulate for the total team effort. However, an individual team member may excel and advance in competition as a champion. Two wrestlers of opposing teams begin by trying to penetrate the other's defenses to gain an advantageous hold position. Each move is calculated to an end of breaking down the opponent and ultimately pinning him to the mat. The struggle continues until the time has expired.

Wrestling is officiated by four officials—one judge, one referee, one mat chairman and one controller. All officials are dressed in white and share responsibilities for scoring and fair play.

DEFINITIONS

Takedown A maneuver by an opponent that results in taking his opposition off his feet and on to the mat.

Headlock A move in which one opponent grips the head of the other in his arm, usually used as a takedown maneuver.

Escape A calculated move by an opponent who is trapped in the grip of his opposition that results in his breaking free or gaining a better position on his opponent.

Pin When one opponent is held on the mat and the referee declares him down for the count. The one who is pinned loses the match.

Without playing experience in these four sports, your understanding may be limited. Reading and digesting sports information is difficult, so review the explanation of game sequences and picture your team as the offense or defense. It is a good idea to watch a game on television where you can study the actions of the teams and officials. Ponder the sports quiz at the end of this chapter to help refresh you on some important facts in sport.

★SOCCER: A LOOK TO THE FUTURE

Soccer is the most popular sport in the world, making the World Cup Soccer Tournament the most widely viewed sporting event. One of the fastest growing competitive sports in America, soccer may become the newest and largest frontier for American cheerleaders.

A soccer match is played between two teams consisting of 11 players each. The match is played on a rectangular field with goals at each end. The match is made up of two periods lasting up to 45 minutes each with only a five-minute halftime break. The game consists of the two opposing teams kicking a ball around strategically to teammates, in an attempt to kick the ball into the opponents' goal net for a score. Nearly all of the ball handling is done with the feet, with some shots with the head; only the goal keeper may use his hands, and only within a designated area.

The kickoff team is the first to go on the offense and begins to pass, with the feet, between teammates toward the other team's goal. If the ball is stolen back, the other team begins to attack in a similar manner. Soccer is a high contact sport and is characterized by non-stop play. With the exception of the five-minute half-time, the only breaks in the game come when a team scores by kicking the ball into the opponents' goal net or the referee stops the game for penalties. Upon a score the game resumes with a kickoff in the same manner as beginning the game.

There are three officials in a soccer match. Two linesmen and one referee, and all share responsibilities for maintaining fair play.

DEFINITIONS

Free Kick A kick awarded to a team that has been fouled as a penalty to the team who committed the foul.

Penalty Kick A kick awarded to a team that has been fouled within the designated penalty area as a penalty to the team who committed a foul. It is more severe than a free kick because this kick is taken in close range of the goal (eleven meters), and is opposed only by the goalkeeper.

Throw In A method of putting the ball back in play after it has been kicked out of bounds or outside the touch line on either side of the field. It is thrown in at the point it left play by the team who did not touch the ball last.

Offside When a player is closer to the opponents' goal than the ball and fewer than two of the opponents' team. The penalty for being off side is a free kick for the opposing team.

Goalkeeper The player assigned to defend the teams' goal area.

Touch line The line making up the outer boundaries of both sides of the playing field.

★ SPORTS QUIZ

1. How many playing periods are there in a football game? A basketball game? A soccer match?

2. What is a first down?

3. What do an interception and a defensive rebound have in common?

4. What is the difference between offense and defense in all sports?

5. How many points is a touchdown? A basketball goal? A hockey goal? A soccer goal?

★ ANSWERS

1. Four quarters in football and basketball, and two halves in soccer.

2. A gain of more than ten yards within a four-down series by an offensive football team or the first play after gaining possession of the ball.

3. They are both turnovers of possession of the ball from the offense to the defense.

4. The offense has the ball and the defense is trying to get the ball.

5. A touchdown is six points, a basketball goal two (or three, depending on the range) points, and hockey and soccer goals are one point.

Cheerleading becomes much more gratifying once you fully understand the rules behind the sport. What better way to have fun and expand your horizons than enjoying the sports most popular in your school? And remember, without sports, cheerleading would not have been created.

★ PART III ★

PREPARATION AND LIFESTYLE

One of the most important considerations in preparing for a tryout or season on a squad is developing a training program that supports both health and fitness. You want to look good, but more importantly you want the flexibility and stamina to fulfill the demands of rigorous routines. Safety is a factor both in training and on the field. If you take the time to warm up and perform movements properly you will greatly reduce the risk of injury. Make your training program complete by taking into consideration all of the many factors that will affect your performance.

To be the best, you must be healthy, believe in your program goals and consistently work towards achieving them. Now, let's get started!

★CHAPTER 5★
NUTRITION

'm too busy to plan for well-balanced meals." "I can't seem to make the time to eat right." "I'll get fat if I eat three times a day." These are the most common phrases I hear among cheerleaders. Combine these food fallacies with a hectic schedule, and it's no wonder we don't eat properly.

When a young woman decides to try out for cheerleader one of the first things she plans to do is go on a diet. We can all agree that a cheerleader should look good. This does not mean, however, that she must use restrictive diets. It simply means that her weight should be proportionate to her height.

Young ladies have high nutritional needs. It is foolish and dangerous to sacrifice health for cheerleading or any other activity.

If you are significantly overweight and want to slim down before tryouts, by all means stick to your goal, assuming you have allowed yourself a reasonable time in which to do so.

It is best to consult a nutrition counselor who can put you on a program designed for your nutri-

tional needs. Avoid fad diets and quick-loss diet foods which will cause you more harm than good. Not only will you regain the weight, you could start yourself on a cycle of roller coaster weight fluctuations that is difficult to break.

A well-planned balanced diet, on the other hand, can help you lose weight gradually and maintain the loss. Manage your weight by eating healthy foods. You don't want to deprive your body of calories and fuel. If you do, your internal motor will run down and so will you. You will actually have more trouble maintaining your weight if you starve yourself from healthy foods.

You may also need to be your own teacher or coach when it comes to nutrition. Many schools do not have any sophisticated concept of diet and exercise. There are actually coaches who suggest the cheerleaders live on one salad per day to maintain performance weight. This is, to put it delicately, nonsense.

Here is a simple rule of thumb. The U.S. Department of Agriculture and the U.S. Department of Health and Human Services suggests that all people follow the Food Guide Pyramid. Everything at the top of the pyramid such as fats and sweets are to be used sparingly. Everything at the bottom of the pyramid, breads and cereals, is to be eaten abundantly, 6–11 servings per day. The milk group requires 2–3 servings, the meat or meat alternative group, 2–3 servings, the vegetable group, 3–5 servings and the fruit group, 2–4 servings.

By making good choices from the largely non-processed foods (i.e., not refined from its original state) suggested by the pyramid, you can eat a lot, maintain your weight and have enough energy to perform at maximum capacity.

Changing your eating habits and thoughts about food will require commitment and education, as does everything else you want to do. If you are sensible you almost can't go wrong. If you want to live on chocolate, potato chips and cola you will have to pay the price. But if being healthy is important to you, there are easy-to-follow eating habits that will serve you well for a lifetime.

Director's Doctrine

The physical requirements placed on you as a cheerleader raise your nutritional needs beyond those of the average person. The foods you eat can greatly influence your level of performance.

Most coaches and sponsors want you to be healthy for your own sake and so you can be a top performer. Since eating right is the basis for building stamina, endurance and overall body tone, they may support you in forming some kind of program for your squad. It may be easier to learn new ways of eating if you do it together.

Nutrition is a serious issue among cheerleaders. In my experience, many of the most successful cheerleaders and dancers lack proper nutrients because of their poor eating habits. They blame it on their "on-the-run" schedules with frequent appearances.

But you can eat well on-the-run by making proper choices. For example, if you have to eat at a fast-food restaurant, order a salad and/or a baked potato. If you avoid rich toppings you have a good, high-fiber meal. Also, many fast food restaurants have grilled chicken, which is much lower in fat than anything fried.

Eliminate your consumption of soda pop or other high-calorie drinks. Water is always the best beverage to consume for your daily requirement of fluid.

You can purchase quick-to-prepare foods at most stores that are low in fat, sugar and sodium.

★ THE BASIC FOOD GROUPS

Proper nutrition involves the day-to-day intake of the five primary food groups and water. The basic food groups are:

Breads and Grains
Fruits
Vegetables
Meats and Protein Alternatives
Milk and Dairy Products

Six Nutrients for Better Health

Six major nutrients make up the basic food groups. Each one serves a different purpose that is necessary for daily life activity. They include the following:

Carbohydrates: Ready energy sources stored in the liver as glycogen. They overcome our sense of fatigue. Complex carbohydrates also contain fiber which is essential to the elimination of waste and toxins from the body.

Fats: Most fats are difficult to use as energy. Your body stores fat as a reserve fuel source.

Minerals: Help to carry out normal cellular functions. They combat muscle cramps and fatigue while speeding recovery from injury.

Proteins: Used for tissue building and repair of muscles.

Vitamins: Act as a catalyst for bodily functions. Most vitamins are found in the foods we eat.

Water: The body is made up primarily of water. You can lose up to five pounds of water during a hard workout. If you drink a minimum of eight glasses throughout the day you will prevent dehydration and cramping. Water is also good for your complexion.

Why do we eat less of all foods when we decide to lose weight? We stop eating properly when we don't know how to balance our food intake. To maintain a healthy weight, carefully select foods to include the six nutrients while minimizing your intake of fat. Your body stores fat very efficiently, so any fat digested contributes to your overall body fat.

Measurements of Body Fat

There are people who are thin but who have too much body fat in proportion to lean muscle weight. Just because you are thin do not assume you are fit. You may be surprised how much fat the body can store.

You can measure the amount of body fat you have in many different ways. If you want to have your body fat measured, you can probably get some help from your coach or local YWCA. There are three methods of testing body fat that are most commonly used, but you should keep in mind that each of these is inaccurate to a point. You should take the same test a week later to see if it is consistent. The three most commonly used methods are:

Skinfold Calipers: Gaining in popularity, the skinfold caliper method measures the amount of skin in a device that "pinches" the skin. It allows the technician to see the percentage of fat measured. Sometimes fat is inaccurately measured, creating a false reading.

Underwater Weighing: More commonly used by those trying to build muscle tissue and mass. This method involves measuring displacement and weight while the subject sits in a tub of water. The measurement is affected by heavy breathing which can produce false readings.

Bio-Electrical Impedance: Extremely rare among cheerleaders, this method is performed by a professional in the field of sports fitness with precision medical instruments to measure electrical resistance. Certain health factors can hinder an accurate reading.

Weight-to-height medical charts are commonly used in middle and high schools, but they are rarely used at the collegiate or professional levels. They are considered too general for most squads. The weight scale is the most common method used to measure weight, *not fat*. It is only used to measure weight changes.

A reminder and word of caution: to become a lean cheerleader does not mean you should use restrictive diets. An exercise program combined with some dietary changes should be enough.

If you are like most people, once you know your body fat percentage, you will either want to hide in your closet or do something drastic. Remember, to lose weight, your body must use more energy than it consumes. This means eating the right foods in smaller portions while getting plenty of physical activity. It is not healthy to skip meals to lose drastic amounts of weight. That weight loss is only temporary, and the pounds will return and increase more once you resume eating again. Proper weight loss should happen slowly. If you must lose weight, lose it correctly and permanently by making good eating choices.

★EATING DISORDERS

Young women who participate in activities that emphasize how they look are particularly prone to eating disorders. Many young people create nightmares in their own minds of how other people perceive them. Under these circumstances it is all too easy to fall prey to a battle with food.

Adult women are also prone to these disorders. The increased pressure on adult performers to maintain a certain weight, particularly when their bodies are maturing, leads to an increase in the number of health problems.

Eating disorders, where food becomes an obsession either through avoidance or addictive behavior, are considered to be part psychological and part chemical. However, if you recognize there is a problem and catch it early, it can be corrected. Talk to somebody you trust. The obsession to be thin can start in grammar school and, if not stopped, will follow a young woman into adulthood.

Eating Disorder Statistics

Research indicates:

> **50%** of fourth-grade girls diet because they think they are too fat.
>
> **90%** of high-school girls diet because they think they are too fat.
>
> Only about **10%** of high-school girls are actually overweight.
>
> **40%** of college-aged women follow diets of 800 calories per day, or less. Semi-starvation is 1200 calories per day.
>
> **14%** of college-aged women vomit at least once in a while in order to control their weight.
>
> **8%** of college-aged women use laxatives at least once in a while as a weight control method.
>
> **100%** of all dieters experience urges to binge eat because they are hungry.

Note: Adapted with permission from *Eating and Exercising Disorders*, by J. B. Rubel, Copyright © 1991, Anorexia Nervosa and Related Eating Disorders, Inc.

The obsessive desire for thinness can lead to several eating disorders. Bouts with food (if not treated) can cause serious medical complications or even death.

When you hear people mention eating disorders, they are usually referring to anorexia, bulimia, compulsive exercise or compulsive eating. All of these disorders are curable with proper treatment and cooperation on the part of the patient.

Carista, a former Dallas Cowboys Cheerleader, describes her experience with obsessive weight control:

> My obsessions with weight began when I was in the ninth grade. I was taking ballet classes and was advancing to a higher level of *pointe*. All the really great dancers were extra thin. At 5'4" and 100 pounds, I was fat compared to them. I weighed myself daily, and if I gained one pound more I would not eat the next day. Looking back, it seems strange. I never had the "excess" weight I was trying to lose. I realize now that I had the normal weight and they were the ones undernourished.

Carista's experience is not unusual. One of the constant issues a cheerleader or dancer faces is proper weight. This issue fades away when you focus on your proper balanced diet.

Bulimia Nervosa
(The Binge-Purge Disorder)

If you think you may be suffering from Bulimia Nervosa, you should familiarize yourself with the following list of characteristic symptoms.

Individuals with this disorder:

Usually restrict eating, making themselves hungry and vulnerable to binge.
Eat a large amount of food quickly.

Prefer high-fat, high-sugar binge foods.

Try to undo a binge by abusing diuretics or laxatives, exercising or vomiting.

Want to eat right but are afraid of becoming fat.

"Cathy, it has come to my attention that you are suffering from bulimia," the cheerleader director said to the young woman, a member of her squad.

Cathy says that she remembers her coach's words as "hitting her like a hammer between the eyes, challenging her basic beliefs that she was doing great." She continues:

I was stubborn and defensive. I told her I was in perfect control of my health. I was insulted and angry. How could my friends have finked on me? Were they jealous of me? Surely, they had to be!

I needed help. I brooded for a while and thought about how much nerve she had to want to help me. I felt as if the wide world was against me. How could I have bulimia? I knew I didn't eat properly, but bulimia? I thought I was in control. I wasn't experiencing many of the side effects, such as depression. If I thought I was looking heavy in my uniform, I would starve myself for two days, having only water to drink. Then, I would go back to eating. I went through this cycle more during the holidays.

I did remember experiencing an uncontrollable craving for something fattening. I had been dieting for four days trying to lose three pounds that I had gained over the Christmas holidays. For four days I tortured myself by not eating. Then it hit me—"Food." I was like a hungry lion eating out of control.

Later, feeling deeply ashamed, I thought about my tight cheerleader uniform. At first, I rationalized, 'Surely my clothes had to be shrinking.' I was terrorized by guilt. The fear of

gaining any extra pounds was more than I could stand. I took laxatives to try to relieve the fullness that I was feeling. (Someone told me it would take off the extra weight fast.) And being such a perfectionist, gaining weight was just unacceptable. I simply did not know the seriousness of my eating madness nor the consequences it had on my body. Thank goodness for people who cared. My coach literally saved my life.

It has been said that bulimia affects approximately 80% of all performers. It is so common because they all want to change themselves quickly without taking the time to consider their health.

In our minds the fastest way to become slim is to stop eating, so we stop. Thinking that we are in control of our life, we go as long as we can until we are starving ourselves.

Then, as though the body is fighting back, we eat everything in sight, feel guilty because we did not stick to our diet, then try to undo our sin of overeating by vomiting or taking diuretics and laxatives. This cycle only becomes more extreme the longer you allow it to happen. You binge and purge, and binge and purge.

The National Association of Anorexia Nervosa and Associated Eating Disorders identifies the term "bulimarexia" as a different illness. This term includes both gorging and purging and occurs more frequently as a part of Anorexia Nervosa or an aftermath.[1]

ANOREXIA NERVOSA
The individual suffering from Anorexia Nervosa also exhibits several distinct symptoms, including:

Keeps weight less than 85% of that expected for height, bone structure and age.

Is obsessed with weighing and measuring food: often separates food on a plate.

Diets even when underweight or alarmingly thin.

Denies anything is wrong.

Note: Adapted with permission from *Eating and Exercise Disorders*, by J. B. Rubel, © 1991, Anorexia Nervosa and Related Eating Disorders, Inc.

Anorexia is similar to bulimia but is characterized by a dramatic weight loss within a relatively short amount of time, usually due to a repulsion against and avoidance of all but the most minimum amounts of food. Anorexics are obsessed with being thin and often believe "you can never be thin enough."

An anorexic has an inner view of herself as fat that conflicts with reality and will possibly avoid taking in any calories at all costs—even the cost of her own life.

Someone is diagnosed as anorexic if she is at least 25% below her normal body weight without any other medical cause.[2]

95% of those suffering from anorexia are female. The disorder will typically appear between the ages of twelve and eighteen.

Anorexia requires intervention. It is psychological in nature but may have a component that is nutritionally based. Some studies show there could be a severe zinc deficiency in anorexics which, rather than being the result of the starvation, may be a factor in bringing on the condition.

It is possible for a young woman to outgrow it, but for many, if left untreated, the condition could have fatal results. It is helpful to catch the condition early. What may be perceived as innocent adolescent concern with body image could be the first step into the clutches of a highly destructive disorder.

COMPULSIVE EXERCISE

Like those suffering from other eating disorders, the individual who is a compulsive exerciser shows certain symptoms of the disorder. Such an individual usually:

Exercises several hours per day, perhaps to justify eating habits.
Defines self-worth in terms of performance.
Is never satisfied with accomplished goals.
May be fanatical about weight.

Here's the story of Desirée, a former Dallas Sidekicks Cheerleader:

I had a real sweet tooth. I convinced myself that a Snickers bar contained far less calories than lunch. When I intended to eat anything else for lunch, I would panic. Afraid of gaining weight, I would run or exercise harder. I set higher and more strenuous exercise expectations to make up for my need to eat more food. I had to look good for the fans. I had to keep improving myself. I became motivated by working off calories so I could eat more food.

Desirée's story is typical. She was addicted to sweets as well as exercise. She felt great when people noticed her hour-glass figure. Looking her best was so important for her that she imposed stiffer and more vigorous exercise demands on herself with each compliment given. Her desire to be perfect had created addictive and obsessive behavior, which she had to counteract through a change of habits and perseverance.

COMPULSIVE OVEREATING

The compulsive overeater similarly exhibits certain signs of suffering from the disorder. This individual:

Eats for several hours at a time.
Usually eats high calorie and high fat foods.

Sally always wanted to try out for the cheerleading squad. A member on the squad told her she should try to lose 15 pounds before tryouts, which were ten weeks away. Sally loved eating high-fat snack foods when she was bored. But she had a habit of snacking all the time. She was embarrassed and troubled by her weight because she was bottom heavy. This gave Sally a low self-image. She tried diets, but failing to lose her goal amount each week, she became tired, frustrated and hungry. The food seemed to console her. Eating for hours at a time, she did not make time for proper meals. By the time try-outs came, Sally's disappointments grew 21 more pounds. She never did try out for the team.

Sally's need to consume large amounts of food for extended periods of time and skipping meals to temporarily satisfy her depression was robbing her body of its daily allowances. Unlike Desirée's eating habits, which were invisible, Sally's eating habits couldn't be missed. Although Sally might have needed intervention by a health professional, she could have been helped in losing those extra pounds simply by deciding to be healthy and by adopting some simple habits.

★ THE TRAINING TRIO

Here are three habits that can help you maintain a healthy weight without too much effort. I call them the "Training Trio."

Only eat when you are hungry,
Never eat after 7 P.M.
Cut out the snacks between meals that keep
   you from eating your regular meals.

It's also a good idea to eat more slowly and chew well, even when you are really hungry. Your stomach needs about 20 minutes to notify your brain that you're full. By eating slower, you will actually eat less without robbing yourself of the proper food groups. Avoid junk food items, too, and you'll see in just a few days that you will not only look better, you will feel better too.

Finally, when you are feeling down and out, try to release the stress by going to a concert or taking a leisurely walk through the park. Entertainment, not food, is the perfect solution for the boredom

blues. And remember, it only takes two weeks to change your eating habits.

★ PHYSICAL MANIFESTATIONS THAT CAN OCCUR IN EATING DISORDERS

Bulimia
Weight fluctuations of 10–15 pounds.
Dependency on diuretics, laxatives, or induced vomiting.
Cavities in the tooth enamel caused by purging.
Fainting spells, severe headaches or dehydration.
Respiratory complications, kidney and liver damage, internal bleeding.
Death.
Anorexia
Dramatic weight loss.
Dehydration, digestive problems, Amenorrhea, liver and kidney complications.
Poor blood circulation.
Degenerating bones and hair, and increased dental problems.
Irregular heart rhythm.
Death.
Compulsive Exercise
Pulled muscles, torn ligaments, or damaged tendons.
Increased bone injury.
Cardiac Arrest.
Death.
Compulsive Overeating
Increasing weight gain.
Fullness or bloating feeling.
High blood pressure, heart attack, or diabetes.

Note: Adapted with permission from *Eating and Exercise Disorders*, by J. B. Rubel, © 1991, Anorexia Nervosa and Related Eating Disorders, Inc.

★ NUTRITION AND YOU

Now, to review your eating habits, you should ask yourself the following questions:

Do you feel you are in a constant battle with food?

Do you use severely restrictive diets?

Do you fear not being able to stop eating voluntarily?

Do you binge eat to relieve stress?

Do you exercise several hours per day to try to justify your eating patterns?

If you answer yes to two or more of the above questions, you may have an eating disorder. I recommend that you seek the guidance of a registered dietitian or nutritionist.

★ VITAMIN SUPPLEMENTS

Those of you who are not yet convinced that a sensible healthy diet is the best thing for you, do not be lured into thinking vitamins may be your salvation. Vitamin supplements are the biggest dietary fad on the open market. Although they may be beneficial in certain contexts, there is no clear scientific proof that vitamin pills are helpful to anyone except those people with a vitamin deficiency. Your body naturally feeds off vitamins it gets from the foods you eat. An overdose of vitamins can acutely poison your system. Unless you become an expert on vitamins, do not use them as a low calorie substitute for eating substantial food. Be sure you get the nutrition your body needs by maintaining a well-balanced diet.

★ PRE-COMPETITION MEALS

Tryouts will be a nervous time for you, so eat something to give your body energy for the per-

formance. Select healthy snacks such as bran muffins, pretzels, celery or carrot sticks, saltine crackers or an apple. These items may be eaten frequently throughout the day to boost energy, and you don't have to feel guilty about eating them.

★ A DIET IS NOT THE ANSWER

Keep in mind that a "diet" is not the answer to anything. Learning to eat properly every day of your life is the key. Read updated nutritional information periodically to advise yourself of any food imbalances you may be experiencing. For more information or literature about eating disorders, refer to Appendix C for a listing of eating disorder associations.

Finally, here are my successful secrets to help you maintain the desired weight you need to become a cheerleader.

CINDY'S SIX SUCCESS SECRETS
- Eat three well-balanced meals, using the basic food groups.
- Avoid high-calorie, high-fat foods and read the labels of packaged foods. Stay away from saturated fats, high-sodium and high-sugar-content foods.
- Consult a registered dietitian or nutritionist before trying a program, especially if it is a diet, or involves taking diet pills.
- Never take short cuts to lose weight. Avoid water pills, laxatives and skipping meals.
- Enjoy the holidays by choosing well. Eat small portions of special foods and go lightly with gravies or rich sauces.
- Be happy with yourself and avoid comparisons with others.

Eating properly will positively change your outlook on life. You will have more energy and your bodily appearance will improve. Restrict your food purchases to healthy foods such as

fresh, color-rich vegetables, like carrots and broc-
coli, and greens. Choose fresh fruit such as
oranges and apples, lean meats, fish and poultry,
low-fat dairy products and whole-grain breads.

Snack on fruits and vegetables when you get
hungry as well as rice cakes, plain popcorn, and
pretzels (low fat, low salt, in moderation.) Soon
you will get into the swing of a healthy eating
lifestyle and junk food will seem very unappeal-
ing. Your weight will quickly zero in at its opti-
mum level and you will look and feel like a winner.

[1] National Association of Anorexia Nervosa and Associated Disorders. Data derived from symptom literature, December 13, 1991.
[2] Center for Study of Anorexia and Bulimia. Data derived from symptom literature, December 5, 1991.

★CHAPTER 6★

STRENGTH AND CONDITIONING

Today's cheerleading demands immense athletic ability. To perform well, your body must be conditioned for the type of activity it will have to endure as a cheerleader. This chapter will help you design a complete training program to improve strength imbalances and develop weak muscles. Instruction in proper technique and basic awareness of the musculoskeletal system will help prevent the most common cheerleading training injuries. Working toward a balance of flexibility, endurance and strength will enable you to achieve the high level of cheerleading performance necessary to excel in competition. The following are benefits for keeping you healthy, in shape, looking and feeling good.

SEVEN BENEFITS OF STRENGTH AND CONDITIONING

Improves motor performance
Develops better range of motion
Tones weak, sagging muscles
Improves muscle imbalances
Elevates metabolism
Decreases body fat
Promotes a healthy mental self-image.

Resistance training for female athletes is a relatively new discipline in the western world. Beginning in the early 1950s with track and field athletes, women's resistance training sought to improve strength and met with good success.[1] To gain a better understanding of conditioning training, we will explore some very basic body bio-mechanics, beginning with the essential building blocks.

★ MUSCLES

Your body has more than 600 muscles. These muscles constitute approximately 30% of an average woman's weight and 40% of an average man's weight.[2] Because of the hormonal differences between male and females, most females can significantly increase their strength and power without bulking up. There is a great amount of data to demonstrate this fact.[3] When females gain more muscle, they will gain body weight. You should not be afraid of this weight gain; as you build stronger muscles you will decrease your percentage of body fat. You will actually look more slender and in better shape, because your body will look smooth and toned. Muscles are the building blocks for improving flexibility, power and strength. When you begin to exercise on a daily basis you will notice greater muscle tone and size. Muscles are divided into three groups:

Cardiac muscle: This muscle drives the heart; its conditioning determines our level of endurance. It may be conditioned directly.

Smooth muscles (involuntary): These muscles work automatically without our having to think about moving them. Many of these muscles contribute to our level of endurance and may be conditioned indirectly.

Skeletal muscles (voluntary): These muscles are controlled by our command and determine our strength, power and level of flexibility.[4]

Cheerleader Musculoskeletal System

We will concentrate on developing your voluntary muscles and cardiac muscle. In doing so, you will condition the involuntary muscles to prepare them for the rigorous activity of cheerleading. But first, let's get the answers to some basic questions. Many questions go unasked when a young man or woman begins a training program for the first time, simply because there is no one to discuss the subject with him or her personally.

Questions and Answers

Dr. Joseph A. Butts, M.D., Orthopedic Surgeon and Sports Medicine Specialist at the Institute of

Sports Medicine and Rehabilitation, based in the Houston area, answers the following questions.

Why should muscles be stretched prior to exercise?
　　Muscles are made of a large number of fibers, many with thin, elastic-type properties. The resting length of the fibers is less than the functional length and stretching before exercise will effectively increase the length of the muscle fibers slightly and thus decrease the likelihood of muscle strain or injury. If you take a rubber band and stretch it too hard or too fast, it will either lose its elasticity or rupture. But if you take a rubber band that is a little longer, it will take more force to cause it to lose its elasticity or rupture.

Do muscles turn to fat when they are not worked regularly?
　　Muscles do not turn into fat when not worked out. As the muscle is worked less, the numbers of

muscle fibers do not decrease, but the sizes of the fibers do. As you use the muscles less, you will burn fewer calories. If your intake of calories remains the same but the use of those calories decreases, the body will try to find a way to store those unused calories for future use. One of the body's favorite ways is to store excess calories in the form of fat, and one of its favorite places to store fat is between muscle fibers.

Should getting into shape be painful?

Some muscle aches and pains are a natural part of the conditioning process. However, there should not be a great deal of pain associated with getting into shape. There is always the production of some waste products that can cause muscle soreness following exercise. Additionally, there is the chance of some minor muscle strains or ligament sprains during exercise, as well as minor muscle cramps. However, the natural discomfort associated with conditioning should not last for more than several hours after the exercise. If you are sore for a day or two after the exercise, you are progressing too quickly and need to back off on how rapidly you are increasing intensity of the conditioning program.

What causes sore muscles?

There is no one cause of muscle soreness. If the soreness lasts for just an hour or two following the exercise period, it was probably the result of waste products such as lactic acid which are natural by-products of a working muscle. If there is muscle cramping or spasm such as a charley horse, it is probably the result of dehydration. It is best to treat dehydration by drinking plenty of fluids (best choice is water). Occasionally, muscle cramping is the result of an electrolyte imbalance. This occurs more frequently in people who neglect a reasonable dietary intake for an extended period of time. Without any dietary master's degree, you can supplement your diet by eating foods that are good for you, such as bananas. Muscles that are sore for longer than several hours after the exercise are a sign that you are doing too much.

What is the role of a physical therapist?

There are three facets of sports medicine. Our major goal is to prevent an injury from occurring in the first place. To this end, we stress proper conditioning, including strength, flexibility and joint range of motion, as well as proper technique and equipment. If an injury does occur, we then try to decrease the amount of swelling as well as trying to maintain as much strength flexibility and joint range of motion as possible. The third facet of sports medicine is rehabilitation of the injured area and the body in general to decrease the likelihood of reinjury. The therapist helps design and carry out an exercise program for the prevention, treatment and rehabilitation of athletic injuries.

Should you be unfortunate enough to experience an injury that requires rehabilitation, a physical therapist recommended by your physician will help you on an appropriate workout program. The physical therapist will guide you to recovery in the quickest and safest way possible.

★ WARM UPS AND COOL DOWNS

Warm ups are the alarm clocks that awake your muscles for work. They elevate body temperature, promoting circulation by increased blood flow. Warm ups are best performed with a warm-up suit on. Jogging in place, riding the exercise cycle, jumping rope or practicing straddle hops are excellent starters for your warm-up routine. When a light sweat becomes noticeable, you should begin stretching all the muscle groups you plan to use during the workout or practice session.[5]

Cool downs put your muscles back into a normalized state. Following a vigorous workout, a relaxing cooling-off period is imperative for decreasing post–workout muscle aches and stiffness. Gradually let your body adjust to a lower heart rate with easy exercise, then continue with light stretching. A proper cool down will help circulate the blood and alleviate lactic acid build up.[6] Complete warm ups and cool downs will greatly decrease the pain of growing muscle and reduce your chances of injury.

★ FLEXIBILITY

Flexibility is defined as the capability of muscles and joints to move through a full range of motion . The five main flexibility points are hip joints, knees, ankles, lower back and shoulders.[7] Always stretch and exercise the largest muscles first. Begin with your legs, then back, abdominals, arms and neck. Incorporate this habit into your training regimen. Begin with slow, held, positions and *try not to bounce or jerk to your position*. Improper technique and overstretching can cause an acute or chronic musculoskeletal injury. Hold each stretch position for fifteen to thirty seconds and repeat if necessary. Flexibility stretching is the final element in warm ups and cool downs.

Key Flexibility Exercises

Head to Toe Rotations

PURPOSE: To relax joints for greater mobility.

Starting Position:

1. Stand and relax shoulders and arms. Comfortably lean head forward and slowly circle head around. Repeat in opposite direction.

2. Stand and place arms down at side. One at a time, circle shoulders forward and down several times. Repeat together.

3. Windmill arms over your head and in front of you as if you are swimming. Repeat in opposite direction. Circle wrists one at a time and then together.

4. Standing tall, bend chest slightly forward and circle trunk around.

5. Stand with feet shoulder-width apart and bend knees. Circle hips slowly around. Repeat in opposite direction.

6. Stand and lift one leg off ground. Point toe and slowly circle ankle from foot. Change directions. Repeat steps with flexed foot. Change legs and repeat steps.

7. Standing tall and straight, gently rise up on to your toes then press heels back down to floor. Repeat several times.

Stork

PURPOSE: Stretch quadriceps.

Starting Positions:

Beginner—Use a chair to support your weight. Stand upright in straight alignment. Hold chair with one hand and lift leg back and grasp toes with opposite hand. Gently press heel toward buttocks. Hold for 15 seconds. Exchange legs and repeat.

More Difficult—Lift leg back and grasp toes with both hands. Gently press heel toward buttocks. Hold for 15 seconds. Exchange legs and repeat.

Standing Chest to Knees

PURPOSE: Stretch hamstring muscles

Starting Position: Assume standing position with feet together. Keeping legs straight, slowly bend forward over knees and place palms on floor. Hold stretch for 20–30 seconds without bouncing.

Standing Chest to Leg

PURPOSE: Stretch hamstring and calf muscles

Starting Position: Stand with feet shoulder-width apart. Turn right leg out and keep straight while bending left leg. Flex right foot at the ankle and gradually place chest to leg. Hold 20–30 seconds. Return to standing position. Repeat steps with left leg.

Straddle Lunge

PURPOSE: Stretch hamstring muscles

Starting Position: Stand with feet wide apart. Keeping hips squared to front, bend right leg and gently shift weight to right side position. Support weight by placing palms on floor at center. Your legs should form a straight line from your hip joint to your toes. Hold stretch for 15 seconds. Repeat steps to left side.

Straddle Point-Flex Series

PURPOSE: Stretch hamstrings and calf muscles

Starting Position: Assume straddle position. Keep back straight, legs straight and hips squared to front. Point toes and gently raise arm over head to stretch over the shoulder. Hold stretch for 15 seconds. Turn torso towards leg and place chest at knee. Hold 15 seconds. Turn to center and place chest to ground. Hold 30 seconds. Progress to other leg and stretch chest to knee for 15 seconds. Turn torso away and raise arm over the shoulder to stretch. Hold 15 seconds. Repeat with feet in flexed position.

Leg Raise
PURPOSE: Stretch hamstring muscles

Starting Position: Lie flat on your back with feet in flexed position. Slowly raise leg as high as you can towards head until you feel a comfortable stop. Keeping your legs straight and your back flat, hold stretch for 30–60 seconds. You may

choose to grasp the ankle of your raised leg for a better stretch. Repeat steps with pointed toes. Change legs and repeat sequence.

Knee to Chest
PURPOSE: To limber back and hip muscles

Starting Position: Lie flat on back. Keeping left leg straight, slowly raise right knee to chest. Hold for 15 seconds. Change legs and repeat.

Hip Flexor Stretch
PURPOSE: Limber hip flexor mobility

Starting Position: Assume stag lying position. Keep toes pointed and back to floor. Slowly roll stag leg to side. Hold 15 seconds. Return to starting position, change legs and repeat steps.

Press Ups

PURPOSE: Stretch lower back, chest and abdominal muscles

Starting Position: Lie flat on stomach placing hands on the floor by shoulders. Gently press up and straighten arms. Keep pelvis and legs on floor. Hold stretch for 30 seconds. Repeat one time.

★ STRENGTH

To increase muscle strength, fatigue or "overload" must take place. A muscle has to be worked to become fatigued: a condition some coaches refer to as stress-failure. Strength training may involve the use of your body weight, free weights or machines. Resistance training can target weak muscles or imbalances. Strength training programs use methods for isolating a resistance force on a muscle group, thereby causing it to fatigue or overload.

"No pain, no gain" is unfortunately the way it will be when you begin building muscle. But don't confuse growing pains with sharp warning pains. Growing pains do not feel sharp; they feel like a tired ache. Eventually your growing pains will end and your muscle strength will increase.

Significant medical evidence has shown that as you increase muscle strength, you decrease your chances of becoming injured.

Key Strengthening Exercises

Squats

MUSCLES DEVELOPED: Thighs and buttocks

Starting Position: Stand with feet shoulder-width apart. Keep knees in alignment with toes and extend arms out in front of you, level with the floor. Keeping your back straight, hold chest up and inhale as you squat into a sitting, 90° angle. Exhale and return to standing position. Repeat several times.

Lunges

MUSCLES DEVELOPED: Hips , thighs and buttocks
Starting Positions:

Beginner—Use a chair to support your weight. Stand with one leg in front of the other. Keeping your hips squared and knees above your toes, slowly lean out to front leg. Keep your knee directly over your foot. Change legs and repeat several times.

More Difficult—Perform steps without chair, placing palms on the leg to create resistance.

Crunches

MUSCLES DEVELOPED: Abdominal muscles

Starting Position: Lie on back with knees bent. You can extend your arms in front of you or place them behind your head. Tighten your abdominal muscles simultaneously as you raise your head and neck. Raise off the ground 2–3 inches. Return to floor. Repeat several times.

Straddle Leg Lifts

MUSCLES DEVELOPED: Thigh muscles and quadriceps

Starting Position: Sit in open straddle position. Place hands in front of you, close to your body. Keep your back straight, raise your right leg up. Hold for 10 seconds. Change legs and hold. Rise both up and hold. Repeat sequence several times.

"V" Sit-Ups

MUSCLES DEVELOPED: Abdominal muscles

Starting Position: Assume sitting position with bent knees. Place arms behind you with fingertips facing away from your body. Keeping your back straight, simultaneously raise legs and stretch arms out. Repeat several times.

Leg Weight Series

(Be sure to talk to your physician before starting a weight program!)

MUSCLES DEVELOPED: Back, hip, thigh, buttock and abdominal muscles.

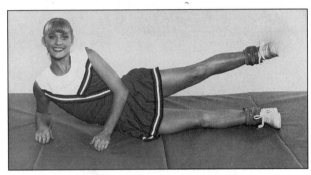

Starting Position:

1. Assume position and rest body on forearms. Slowly raise leg up and down several times.

2. Rest body on side. Place forearm flat on mat. Slowly raise leg up 2–6 inches and return down. Repeat motion several times.

3. Rest body on forearm and hip. Place palms flat on floor. Cross leg over straight leg. Slowly lift straight leg up 1–2 inches off ground and bring down. Repeat several times.

4. Lie on stomach with chest propped up on forearms. Keeping pelvis on the ground, stiffen straight leg and slowly raise from hip 1–2 inches from the floor. Return down to floor. Repeat several times. Exchange legs and repeat steps 1—4.

★POWER

Power is the *maximum* amount of force you can apply towards a resistance. The amount of power you have is best described as a combination of endurance, strength and your reflex readiness. Power is needed in cheerleading to achieve greater height and form when performing jumps, stunts, gymnastics and dance. The power in your legs dictates the height you are able to leap from a standing position. It is your ability to propel your body in any given direction. How high can you jump from a standing position? Power is important to cheerleading, for the more power you build, the more of an asset you will be to a squad.

Key Power Exercises

Straddle Jumps

PURPOSE: To increase speed and height
Starting Position: Stand tall in good postural position. Bending at the knees, push off with toes and jump high into the air. Keeping knees over the toes, land in straddle position first on the balls of your feet then press the heels to the floor. Avoid hyperextending your back as you jump. Repeat several times. Concentrate on controlling each jump.

Jumps in Place

PURPOSE: To increase height.
Starting Position: Stand with feet slightly apart. Jump as high as you can using your arms for momentum. Land in a squat position.

Standing Broad Jump

PURPOSE: To increase height and distance.
Starting Position: Stand tall with feet slightly apart. Simultaneously, bend knees and swing arms back. Jump forward. Measure your jump each time for progress.

★ENDURANCE

Endurance or stamina conditioning prepares your muscles to respond to a required program or activity level. It is gauged by your cardiovascular system's capacity to maintain a specific workload. Stamina is important in cheerleading because the more your heart is conditioned, the longer you will be able to perform without feeling tired. Your high endurance level will help keep you looking and feeling fresh on the sidelines.

Key Endurance Exercises

Straddle Hops

Starting Position: Stand tall with feet shoulder-width apart. Keeping left leg straight, bring right knee up and hop on left leg. Land on ball of foot, pressing down to heel. Change legs and repeat several times.

Push Ups

Starting Position: Lie face down and tuck toes under. Place arms by chest, palms down with fingertips forward. Keep your body straight, rise to upright position and straighten arms. Bend arms and return to floor. Repeat several times.

Tips for Improving Endurance:

Increase time of bike riding, rope jumping, stair climbing or jumping jacks.
Practice endurance exercises to the fullest.
Increase difficulty once per week by adjusting the tension on machines, or by performing more sets.

★YOUR WORKOUT PROGRAM

Before you begin a workout program, you should determine if you are physically fit. In order to do this, you should:

1. Visit your doctor for a physical check-up first. Your doctor can determine your present health.

2. Assess your present position by conducting cardiovascular tests through timed running or the exercise cycle.

3. Test your strength with weight increments or measured resistance machines. Keep a chart. It's fun to see your progress!

What will a workout program do for you? Well-trained muscles burn fat and calories more quickly than unconditioned muscles. For example, your metabolism increases when you begin a daily training regimen, thereby burning calories and fat. As you increase and tone muscle mass, your body-fat percentage will decrease more efficiently. Here is a simple rule of thumb:

Low body fat—More calories burned during a thirty minute workout.
High body fat—Fewer calories burned during a thirty minute workout.

For starter training, perform one set of 8 to 12 repetitions. Be realistic and patient when starting up. Many people give up at the first sign of muscle soreness. Begin slowly, then gradually work toward 12–15 repetitions, but no more. Progression by modest steps will help ease you into a safe but effective conditioning program. If using a machine or free weights, start with little or no weight first, then gradually add weight. Lifting heavy weights fewer times will increase strength. Lighter weights and more repetitions increases desirable endurance, muscle tone and definition. Use free weights only under strict, qualified supervision.

Now let's look at my Sixty Minutes for Sixty Days Workout Program.

★ SIXTY MINUTES FOR SIXTY DAYS

(15 minutes warm up—30–45 minutes workout—15 minutes cool down)

I. Begin your warm up first with jumping rope, running in place or riding the exercise cycle for 1–2 minutes. Then do the straddle hop for 30 seconds. Begin flexibility stretching starting with the legs. Continue stretching the rest of your body until your muscles feel loose and warm.

II. (Monday–Friday, three days per week) After stretching, begin your strengthening and power exercises. Start with the largest muscles first. Perform 8–15 repetitions and proceed through full range of motion. Beginners can start with 1–2 sets.

III. (Monday–Friday, two days per week) After stretching, begin with your endurance exercises for five sets a piece, followed by fifteen to thirty minutes of cheer, dance or gymnastic combination technique practice. You will learn these practices in the next few chapters. When first starting out, it is important to concentrate only on cheer, dance or gymnastics during each session rather than all three during practice. This focus will give you more technique practice time. Alternate each training session.

IV. For strengthening weight exercises, focus on mastering proper technique before adding additional weight or sets. Reduce weight or repetitions instead of sacrificing correct alignment. Practicing perfect form will decrease the chances of undue stress on your body that can result from improper alignment. Be sure to complete each set correctly without cheating. Try lowering the weight or reducing repetitions if technique or correct form is a problem. Once you have mastered 15 repetitions and can repeat them with ease, try adding weight or adding a third set of 10 repetitions. When doing weight training, it is best to add weight in increments of 5 lb. Pause approximately 30–60 seconds between repetitive sets.

V. Remember to lower your heart rate by cooling down. You may use some of the same relaxation and flexibility exercises you used to warm your body up.

You will begin to notice positive results in two and a half to six weeks. Don't give up or give in to sore, tired muscles! It's easy to want to quit when our muscles get sore. The soreness will go away as long as you continue your training. You will be surprised at how much you improve in just two weeks. In sixty days you will look and feel like a different person.

Preteen Training

If you are under the age of fourteen, do not engage in weight training without proper supervision. There are many safety concerns regarding injury that can cause chronic pain, or even disfiguration that I believe offset the practical strength increases.[8] Recent studies indicate strength increases in adolescents with weight training under close supervision. If you or your parents are determined for you to use weights, please note that the National Strength and Conditioning Association recommends 6 repetitions in a set for adolescents.[9] Keep in mind that all weight for this age group must be closely supervised.

★ WEATHER CONDITIONING

Because cheerleading training begins in early summer, you will need to condition yourself for both the heat and cold. Extreme weather distorts your body's ability to dissipate heat normally. Both hot and cold weather are dangerous and adversely effect your performance.

Heat Acclimation

The body has to dissipate much more heat during high temperatures to prevent thermal injury. Cheerleading provides a high-risk environment for thermal injury during the hot months because it requires such long periods of continuous activity without breaks. Start slowly with light exercise in hot weather. After you feel more comfortable, build up to a moderate exercise of 2 hours per day for 15 hot days. You will notice measurable changes in the following: lower body temperature at rest, lower skin temperature at exercise, decreased exercise heart rate and metabolism and increased sweating and evaporative cooling.

Take caution to prevent heat stroke by warming up in the shade. Wear loose clothing that breathes. Drink plenty of fluids before and during exercise to avoid dehydration. Try drinking a minimum of 8 ounces of water or sports drink every twenty minutes.[10]

Cold and Rain

Cold weather and rain are important environmental factors to overcome in cheerleading.

Unfortunately, not every stadium has a dome for protection. As the season progresses from fall to winter, the weather will become a factor in your ability to perform. Body-heat conservation will help you to battle the harsh cold weather that comes late in the season.

Take extra care warming up, and stay warm until immediately before the game. Guard against the wind by wearing added protective clothing. Take extreme care to prevent frostbite, which may affect your fingers and toes without your becoming aware of it. Check your squad members and yourself regularly during those blustering days of winter. Immediately after the event, take action to prevent hypothermia by covering yourself with a warm blanket or coat and removing any wet clothing immediately. Hypothermia is a condition where restricted blood flow to the body's core temperature can be fatal. Hypothermia occurs when the body releases too much heat and causes the temperature to drop far below 98° F.[11]

★ SAFE WORKOUTS

THREE INJURY PREVENTION TIPS

1. Execute proper technique through full range of motion.

2. Warm up and cool down before and after each workout.

3. Heed warning signals.

WORKOUT WARNING SIGNALS

Stop if you feel sharp pain.
Stop if you feel dizzy or lightheaded.
Stop if you feel nausea.

You should seek an overall balance of flexibility and strength. Joints that are too flexible are subject to dislocation and muscles that are too tight are in danger of muscle strain.

Helpful Hints

Here are some hints to get you started on a solid conditioning program that you can maintain over the long haul.

First see your doctor for a medical exam.

Seek a trainer to help define your goals and limits.

Set reasonable expectations.

Always start your program fresh.

Begin slowly. Don't overwork yourself the first day. Gradually work up to a challenging level.

Always start with a warm up to stimulate blood circulation.

If you are working with weights, start with little or minimal weight first.

Your program should always start with the largest muscles first and gradually progress to the smaller muscles.

Master form with each exercise through full range of motion and complete each set successfully *without* cheating.

Watch for warning signals, including sharp pains, nausea or dizziness.

Master technique with each set before adding weight.

Add weight in increments of 5 pounds.

Incorporate a cool down of flexibility after working out.

Commit yourself to 3–4 days a week.

Find a workout buddy if you feel like quitting.

Don't give in to sore muscles! Focus on the ultimate goal: making the squad.

Be patient with yourself. Don't try to do too much, too fast.

[1] National Strength and Conditioning Association, *Strength Training for Female Athletes*. Lincoln, Nebraska: Position paper, 1990), 3.

[2] Van N. Reinhold, *Complete Encyclopedia of Exercises*. New York: Visual Information Limited, 1981).

[3] *Strength Training*, 10.

[4] *The Human Body on File* (New York: Facts on File, 1983).

[5] Peter Verney, *The Weekend Athlete's Fitness Guide* (New York: Facts on File, 1980), 40.

[6] Ibid., 41.

[7] Reinhold, op. cit., 32.

[8] C. Blimke, Ph.D., *Strength Training the Child Athlete* (Gatorade Sports Science Institute, Institute Report, 1989).

[9] National Strength and Conditioning Association, *Prepubescent Strength Training* (Lincoln, Nebraska: position paper, 1984), 7.

[10] Carl V. Gisolfi, Ph.D., *Preparing Your Athletes for Competing in Hot Weather* (Gatorade Sports Science Institute, Institute Report, 1988).

[11] R. R. Pate, Ph.D., *Tips on Exercising in the Cold* (Gatorade Sports Science Institute. Institute Report, 1990).

SAFETY

Cheerleading has certain risks associated with it. In recent years it has become more athletically challenging than ever before. However, cheerleading and safety do not have to be mutually exclusive.

In the earliest days of cheerleading, there were really no safety restrictions even though the high-flying, free-wheeling thigh pitches and free-falling flips (the trademarks of many early squads) posed much danger to squad members. Performing the stunts required exact precision to carry out the maneuver safely. Many squads were conscious of safety factors, but many were simply lucky that tragedy did not come their way. Cheerleaders just seemed invincible.

It wasn't until one evening during a seemingly normal practice session nearly 100 years after the first cheerleaders walked on the field that the tragedy struck, changing the cheerleading world forever.

Cheerleading was at a peak in risky stunting and other unabashedly dangerous nerve-racking antics. One night while practicing, Janis Thompson, a North Dakota State University senior, became the victim of a tragedy that claimed her precious life when she attempted a "basic" pike dismount. Instead of a proper landing, she took an unexpected twist and landed head first on the field house floor.[1] She slipped into a coma from which she never awoke, and later died.

At the time of the accident, the cheerleading industry did not have any universal guidelines for even the high school squads. Safety was always a concern, but the risks were not always taken as seriously as they should have been.

Many squads practiced unsupervised on concrete floors and without mats. Squads practiced wherever they could get a room and permission to carry out a good practice session. The sorrowful loss of Janis Thompson was a pivotal point for cheerleading. Something had to be done to protect cheerleaders from this ever happening again. Cheerleaders everywhere knew they were no longer invincible. Safety became a primary concern at the forefront of every training session from that night onward. Something positive happened in the midst of sadness and sorrow: something for which every cheerleader should be thankful.

Why am I telling you this unhappy story when you want to get on to the cheerleading? Because it's an important part of our history. It's a part of our legacy where considerable change occurred to make us think about what we are doing, to practice more efficiently. It has helped us become more "safety conscious," and for every accident that does occur, it has prevented at least one tragedy.

Safety standards and guidelines have become much more structured and enforced for daily activity, and even more so for competition. National safety standards have been constructive for cheerleading since their design has been one of careful deliberation on behalf of well-qualified parties. Safety guidelines target preventive measures and redundant procedures, rather than restricting wide spectrums of activity that are characteristic of the discipline.

★ STRICT GUIDELINES

Safety Guidelines

The National Federation of State High Schools Association (NFSHSA) formed the Spirit and Rules Committee in 1988 to develop safety guidelines for interscholastic spirit groups. In 1990 the guidelines became rules. At last we have published, universal guidelines that can apply to all spirit squads and which can serve as an excellent reference for official safety standards.

A few of the stunts and apparatuses banned from high school activities include: spring boards and mini-tramps, pyramids more than two levels high, swan dives, free-falling flips, toe and thigh pitches, knee and split and front drops, tension drops, single-base split catches and tosses from one base to another.[2]

Cheerleading Coach Certification

With cheerleading injuries rising in the 1980s, cheerleading associations quickly responded. They developed programs specifically designed to educate cheerleading coaches and advisors. Virtually all cheerleading associations now offer coach certification programs. Certification entails teaching sponsors a firm knowledge of cheerleading safety, liability concerns, risk management and injury trends necessary for safe squad development.

Among these associations is the American Association of Cheerleading Coaches and Advisors (AACCA). The AACCA is a nonprofit national support organization for the betterment of qualified sponsors, coaches and advisors. Through an educated program and certification process, members actively promote cheerleading interests.

For additional information on how your coach or sponsor can receive certification, write to:

AACCA
P.O. Box 508
Cordova, TN 38018–0508

Safety + Practice = Prevention

If you think an accident could never happen to you, you are wrong. Injuries happen all of the time and they don't discriminate. Though an extracurricular activity, cheerleading stunts are a form of athletics. In many ways, cheerleader stunting has become more dangerous than any other athletic activity. Some stunts are *very* dangerous, and need careful application of correct safety procedures. Proper safety precautions make those inevitable mistakes much more forgiving by *preventing* injury. Practice is for making mistakes and correcting them. Avoid injuries by practicing proper safety guidelines. The two go hand in hand: no ifs, ands, or buts, about it! Guidelines are for your protection to avoid potential injuries.

The success of these guidelines—which are relatively difficult to enforce—depends on the education and motivation of coaches, individuals and squads who use them on a daily basis. Even with the safety awareness campaigns of recent years, the 1992 U.S. Consumer Products Safety Commission Reports showed 14,713 hospital injuries related to cheerleading.[3] That is an injury approximately every thirty minutes. The best solution to this problem is for you to practice with a qualified trainer and spotter. Know your safety guidelines and make a habit out of practicing safety procedures.

★ PRACTICE ATTIRE AND PROVISIONS

Clothing

Start your warms ups in a good jogging suit. For practice, wear clothing that is not restrictive and breathes easily. Some of the new breathing synthetic fabrics look nifty, but may not be appropriate for practice because they become slippery after minimal perspiration and tend to hinder normal catches by your partner and spotters. Rubber workout gear is not healthy and is just another weight-loss gimmick. Shorts and a T-shirt or leotard crop-top will work well. Wear cotton that will allow sweat to evaporate. It is very important you buy a good sports bra for support.

Shoes

Select shoes that are lightweight and will provide stable landings. To minimize the risk of potential twists, wear comfortable shoes with good ankle cushions, arch supports and cushioned, supportive soles. Keep the soles clean of any oily or sticky substances. My advice is to wear them only for practice and performance. If your coach or sponsor requires you to wear them to school with your uniform, be sure to wash off the soles with a mild detergent after each wearing.

Hair

Keep hair away from your eyes. If your hair is long, try pulling it into a pony tail or barrette. Long hair looks attractive, but it's likely to get stepped on during stunts. Keep it up and out of your way to minimize potential problems.

Jewelry

Jewelry, other than eye wear, is inappropriate for cheerleading and has a tendency to fly off easily when you are jumping or stunting. It is very distracting and poses a hazard to you and your teammates. If the squad you're trying out for wears a traditional small piece of jewelry for live performances, wear it in a manner that prevents any risk of injury.

Female Hygiene

Unfortunately for females, the menstrual cycle and sanitary pads create a problem when you wear leotard briefs to practice or as part of the uniform itself. If you plan to wear tampons instead of pads, be careful not to neglect crucial changing times. Avoid embarrassing situations and Toxic Shock Syndrome (TSS) by changing your tampons frequently throughout the day. Remove the tampon immediately if you feel dizzy, nauseated or have a headache. TSS can be fatal.

Gum Chewing

How many times have you stepped on a wad of gum? No one wants to get gum in her hair, clothing or shoes. Gum chewing can cause tooth decay, create a slight overbite, be noisy and even look unattractive. It also inhibits proper vocalization of cheers and sidelines. It may have zip, berry and pizzazz but if swallowed unexpectedly, gum can cause you to choke. As a role model, try to set an example on the squad by not chewing gum; in fact, on some professional squads gum chewing is strictly forbidden on and off the field.

★ PRACTICE FACILITIES

Practice facilities are usually chosen for their convenience instead of their suitability. Just the opposite should be true. Your school gymnasium will have a wood floor that is desirable, but always practice on a large mat whenever possible. Select an area that has good lighting and plenty of room to move. The ceiling should be very high for any partner stunts you may wish to practice. Never practice on cement floors because of the high risk of serious injury and minor shin splints. Practice in the facility at a time when there are no distractions and little noise to diminish your concentration. Check the accessibility to nearby telephones. When it comes to emergencies, the telephone is most valuable.

Safety Spotting

Safety spotting is an essential procedure for learning new stunts. It helps you attempt a stunt through its full motion without getting injured. Spotting entails assisting or being ready to assist the performer(s) through each step. Even when there appears to be no need, some stunts require prevention spotting methods. Carefully assisting the performer, the spotter must remain ready to help break sudden falls.

Spotting may look easy, but there are certain safety techniques the spotter can use to become more effective. Enhance your ability as a teammate by learning the basics. There are three different spotting techniques: assistance spotting, non-assistance spotting and harness spotting. Harness spotting involves the use of a waist belt for advanced gymnastics stunts. All are equally important and, in many cases, involve group spotting. Group spotting requires two or more people to participate in the spotting process.

Spotting is a necessity when practicing high dismounts and other maneuvers that leave you vulnerable to a fall.

THREE SAFETY SPOTTING TECHNIQUES:

1. Assistance Spotting Assistance spotting is necessary when learning a new stunt for the first time. It involves holding the performer through the stunt from beginning to end. With hands-to-body contact, the spotter assures safe execution through the movement. The spotter must be alert and, preferably, physically strong for the activity. Guiding carefully, the spotter is responsible for breaking any hard falls resulting from improper execution of the stunt. To avoid potential injury, conduct spotting on a gym mat. The spotter should continue hands-to-body contact until the stunt is successful.

2. Non-Assistance Spotting Non-assistance spotting involves the careful watching of the stunt as it is being executed. The spotter should remain close, prepared to assist the performer through the motion of the stunt. Only after assistance spotting has helped guide the gymnast to several properly executed stunts should the performer attempt the stunt without physical hands-on contact.

3. Harness Spotting Harness spotting is primarily applied to advanced gymnastic and tumbling maneuvers. The harness involves the use of a belt fixed overhead, or on a trolley held by a rope. It is a great tool for mastering advanced stunts with minimal risk of injury. Use a harness only under the supervision of a qualified trainer.

FOUR SPOTTING TIPS

1. The spotter should assist or be ready to assist the performer through each step to prevent injury.

2. The spotter must be alert and preferably physically strong for the activity.

3. The spotter should focus special attention to the head and upper torso areas.

4. The spotter should stand on the side, where the head and shoulders of the performer are most accessible, and out of the way of the other partners involved in the stunt.

★ FIRST AID

"I knew she was hurt but I didn't know what to do." How many times have you heard someone speak of feeling helpless in the face of an injury incident? It's unfortunate that first aid techniques are not known by everyone. This first aid segment is not meant to take the place of a first aid course or manual, both of which are beyond the scope of this work. It is included solely to increase your awareness of basic procedures and point out potential shortcomings in your program.

Minor Injuries:

Be sure to keep a first aid kit and manual nearby for emergencies. Treat minor injuries and bleeding immediately. Rinse off open wounds with cold water and apply pressure to stop the bleeding. Apply an ice pack to bruises and sprains. Use an elastic wrap, and elevate to reduce swelling.[4] If swelling continues, consult your physician for treatment. A more severe sprain could suggest injury to the ligaments.

Major Injuries:

Major injuries can be possible broken bones other than back and neck, or small cuts that require stitches. Major injuries should only be treated by a trained medical professional. Be sure to keep a current list of emergency numbers with your first aid kit and manual by the telephone. Call medical assistance immediately for the nearest emergency center.

Life-Threatening Injuries:

Life-threatening injuries require immediate Emergency Medical Service (EMS) attention. Here are example emergency situations:

1. Broken bones: For joint dislocations and fractures, do not move the limb but elevate if possible to reduce swelling. Never move an injured person, especially if neck, back or head injury is suspected. Only cover them with a blanket to help reduce risk of shock until help arrives.[5]

2. Bleeding: There are two types of wounds: abrasions and open lacerations. Apply firm pressure directly to laceration or puncture wounds using the palm of your hand and a clean cloth. Cold water will be most effective on abrasions unless bleeding is profuse.

3. Contusions: Gently apply ice pack directly on the bruised area and elevate. Remain in a relaxed position.

4. Muscle Tears: Do not move area. Apply ice and elevate.

5. Convulsions: You must keep the person from swallowing the tongue with a flat object or with two fingers that can be placed on top of the tongue to keep the throat open. If breathing stops, pull the mouth open and check to see if the throat is obstructed.

For more details on how to apply proper first aid, read *The American Red Cross First Aid and Safety Handbook,* by Kathleen A. Handal, M.D., and The American Red Cross. Not only will the book answer all of your questions about first aid, but it will also provide you with a working knowledge of handling emergency situations.

CPR CERTIFICATION

Cardiopulmonary Resuscitation (CPR) is a method used on an individual whose pulse and breathing have stopped. Every squad should have one person at practice who is CPR trained and preferably certified. For information on how you can learn CPR, contact the American Heart Association, The American Red Cross or your local Emergency Medical Service or Fire Department for details on first aid training and CPR certification. Your knowledge could save a life.

INJURY ASSESSMENT

The event of an injury may require you to speak to paramedics over the phone or guide first aid application. It's possible that the life of someone who is special to you may depend on how well you perform this task. To make the task of injury assessment easier to remember, try to memorize the Who, What, When, Where, How and Why Method.

1. Who is hurt? State name, age and gender.

2. What was the person doing when the injury occurred? Countless circumstances can lead to injury. Your description should provide a good mental picture of the situation or maneuver performed and how the person injured herself.

3. When did the accident occur? State whether it is a recurring condition or a new injury.

4. Where did the injury take place? Give the operator the full address and location.

5. How serious is the injury? This is the most important determining factor during assessment.

Here are some basic steps to assessing the injured person's condition.

- *What is the injured person's condition?*
  - Is the injured person conscious?
  - Is she/he breathing?
  - Is her/his heart beating?
  - Is there any gross deformity?
  - Is there bleeding?
  - Is there injury to the head or neck?
  - Are there convulsions, nausea or abnormal body temperature? (i.e., cold sweats or chills)
  - Is she/he able to wiggle toes and fingers?
- *Is an ambulance needed?*
  The previous questions should help you determine if an ambulance is needed.

Here are two types of injuries:

- *Minor injuries*: Scrapes, sprains, and bruises do not need an ambulance.
- *Severe injuries*: Stopped breathing and unconsciousness, disfigurement, head and neck injury, numbness, the inability to move freely, and profuse bleeding all signal that an ambulance is needed immediately. If you have any doubt, stay calm and call 911 and describe the situation and symptoms. Let the operator know whether artificial respiration or CPR is being administered. Take instructions from the operator.

- *What should be done until medical assistance arrives?*
  Do your best to keep spectators away. Remain calm and responsible. Stay on the line with the Emergency Medical Services until you have given the operator all the needed information. Let the injured person know medical assistance is on the way. Do not move the injured per-

son. If there is bleeding, apply pressure to the wound. Cover the person with a blanket to prevent shock. Keep the injured person calm while you monitor vital signs. Look for pulse, skin changes and shock symptoms such as cold sweats and pale skin. When shock occurs, the injured will immediately weaken due to unsteady blood pressure. Do not leave the person alone. Wait for medical attention to arrive.

6. Why did it happen? An analysis: How could it have been prevented? Always be in the position to learn from mistakes. It's easy to point the finger of blame when we're scared, but try to learn how to keep the incident from recurring.

EMERGENCY PLAN

Emergency plans are easy to prepare and priceless when needed. Find out if your squad has a safety plan for emergencies. If so, tape it to the designated emergency telephone. Ask the cheerleading coach to schedule an emergency drill as soon as practice opens for the new season. Remember, your concern will display responsible behavior.

SAFETY AWARENESS CHECKLIST

Always warm up before any type of athletic activity.

Do not start squad practice sessions without direct supervision.

Do not try a new stunt without proper training; be sure a qualified instructor and adequate spotters are present.

Practice in a well-lighted area away from noise and distractions.

Have an emergency plan on hand at every practice, even when training at home.

Know your emergency drill by heart.

Do not practice on concrete or wet surfaces.

Heed warning signs

To each of us, safety seems irrelevant when everything is going fine. Think about all the great things you take for granted. Not practicing good safety procedures can change all those things and rob you of those special times with your friends. Actually, it is one of the very few things that can rob you of your dreams. Cheerleading begins with safety. Don't let a preventable situation take you unexpectedly. Remember, practice smart, and you'll cheer for years.

[1] A. Frankel, "Is cheerleading getting too dangerous?" *Seventeen* 46: 56.
[2] National Federation of State High School Associations, *Spirit Rules* (Kansas City, Missouri: NFSHSA, 1993), 7–14.
[3] U.S. Consumer Product Safety Commission. *Neiss Product Summary Report* (Washington, D.C.: U. S. Government Printing Office, 1993).
[4] K. Handal, M.D., *The American Red Cross First Aid and Safety Handbook* (Boston: Little, Brown, 1992).
[5] Ibid., 22.

★ PART IV ★

MASTERING THE BASICS

There are basic skills which form the foundation of your entire cheerleading career. Your mastery of these skills will be a determining factor in your success as a cheerleader. In my case, perfecting the basics was an on-going process throughout the many levels of my development. I have practiced for many hours learning and polishing various skills to increase my range as a beginner, and later as a professional. If you give it everything you've got in the earlier stages, it will come easier for you in the long run.

Remember these three *P*'s: Patience, Practice and Perfection. Be patient with yourself, practice 110% and perfection will not be out of your reach.

CHAPTER 8

CHANTS AND CHEERS

Chants and cheers are organized yells that encourage fan support and participation whether the team is winning or losing. These yells also involve the use of synchronized motions which are entertaining to watch and a lot of fun to do. The synchronized motions usually use both arms and legs. They may be rhythmic, precision or a combination of both.

The synchronized motions are an essential part of leading the crowd in unison. They generate energy which directs the crowd's focus to a particular game event or situation. There is nothing more powerful than a stadium full of roaring fans after points are scored.

Cheers and chants generate excitement. They unite the crowd into a form of team-centered camaraderie. They keep everyone motivated and are crucial for keeping the crowd under control, in good spirits and supportive under all game situations.

THE FUNCTIONS OF CHANTS AND CHEERS
Chants and cheers have four main functions.

1. To capture the crowd's attention and divert unruly behavior. (Like throwing rotten tomatoes when you think there has been a bad call.)

2. To fuel audience enthusiasm, support and good sportsmanship.

3. To draw organized and positive crowd responses.

4. To promote certain game play activity.

Chants

An integral part of cheerleading, chants are short repetitive yells that bolster audience participation. Often referred to as "sidelines," chants call for extra effort from the team and fans alike. They differ from cheers because they are performed continually during a game. Chants mirror game play situations and may be used in place of cheers. Each chant is repetitious in nature, and many different chants can be performed during a game.

For example, entirely different chants are appropriate during a football game when the team is (1) defending a goal line, (2) going for a first down or (3) lining up for a field goal.

There are many generic chants that can be performed at almost any time during the game. A generic chant is anything that does not relate to a particular event in the game, for example:

EXTRA EXTRA
Extra, Extra
We have might
We are Number 1
We are out of sight!

There are three different types of crowd involvement chants:

1. **Repetitions** A word or short phrase that is repeated after the cheerleaders.

2. **Crowd yell contests** The home audience competes in a yell with the visiting audience or against different groups among themselves.

3. **Spectator chant and sing along** A short word or phrase that is performed in unison with the cheerleaders.

You can diversify your "sidelines" by incorporating these three types of chants into your game plan. Upbeat and different, chants keep the adrenaline flowing through the audience from start to finish of each game.

Cheers

Cheers are similar to chants, except they are performed only during pre-game, post-game, or official breaks throughout the game. They are longer than chants and considered by most as a form of entertainment.

Why are cheers important? Like chants, they encourage support for the team and game activity. Because they are longer and more defined, they grab the audience's attention to something new. That's what makes cheers a powerful motivational tool. There are two kinds of cheers:

1. **Concise** Concise cheers are usually performed during short breaks such as time outs. Because breaks come unexpectedly, you can squeeze many of these cheers into a game.

2. **Extended** Extended cheers are excellent choices for longer, defined breaks such as half time and quarter changes.

Both chants and cheers use synchronized motions and yells that prompt the audience to respond.

★ PROTOCOL

There are certain times when chants and cheers are wonderful and other times when they are inappropriate. Here is a helpful rule of thumb so you can avoid embarrassing situations:

CHANT OR CHEER:
At the start of the game as your team reaches the playing field or court
Immediately as a welcome to the visiting team
When your team scores
When your team, or a player on your team, makes an outstanding play
When a player change or substitution has taken place
To show support and good sportsmanship after an injured player leaves the game

DO NOT CHANT OR CHEER:
When a player is hurt

When a penalty is called

When the opposing cheerleaders have started a cheer

When a player is attempting a free throw or the quarterback is calling signals for a play

While the band is playing or important messages are being made over the PA system

When an opposing team member or cheerleader does something humiliating

A conscientious cheerleader understands the responsibility of leading in a sportsmanlike manner. For everyone's benefit and the reputation of your squad. Chants and cheers should always be performed during appropriate moments of the game and must never encourage negative or unsuitable reactions.

★ HOW TO RAISE MOTIVATION

What's a cheerleader to do when the team is losing without the possibility of a win? "It's hard to be happy when your team is losing," says Leslie Ratley, former Spirit Leader for the McCallum Knights cheerleading squad in Austin, Texas. "It's no fun seeing your team getting creamed, but I've found the best way to keep spirits up is to perform the yells the crowd likes the most."

Fans look to cheerleaders for entertainment when their team is struggling. Cheerleaders also serve as damage control. Have you looked closely at a passionate fan when his or her team is losing? Not a pretty sight. Cheering diffuses unsportsmanlike hostility, a malady to which all true fans can be prone, and replaces it with a sense of hope and enthusiasm.

When you perform favorite yells, everyone begins to have a good time again.

With a little innovative thinking, it becomes easier to control the mood of crowd and influence the outcome of the game. Players are as prone to defeatism as anyone else. As much as they try, they can be psyched out by bad audience morale.

Here are three simple Crowd Motivation Techniques:

1. Perform crowd involvement chants and cheers. Get as many people as you can to actively participate.

2. Use visual aids such as signs and cue cards

3. Perform a pom routine, stunts and gymnastics which will draw everyone's attention.

When the team is losing you have to turn on the charm. The audience will look to you for leadership, entertainment and fun. You may be asked to create your own cheer or chant for tryouts. Take into consideration your potential role of fan motivator and see what great ideas you can come up with on your own.

★ MOTIONS

Motions are your visual communication. Most chants are performed rhythmically by hopping from one foot to the other as if prancing in place. Basic arm movements may be performed in 45° and 90° angles or fully extended placements. There are three basic hand positions and three basic foot positions. The basic hand positions are: fist, blade and—more common for routines—jazz. The basic foot positions are: pointed, flexed and regular placement.

There are many different arm motions: hands at hips, daggers, verticals, high "V"–90° angle, low "V"–90° angle, horizontals, diagonals and "K." The following represent basic motions and motion modifiers. Carefully analyze each pictured motion before you begin practicing.

ARM AND HAND MOTIONS

Hands at Hips

Daggers

Vertical Up (Touchdown)

High "V"

Diagonal

"K"

Horizontal "T"

Low "V"

Vertical Down
(Low-Touchdown)

LEG AND FOOT POSITIONS

Straddle

Dig

Lift

Stag

Lunge

After learning each motion, try displaying different positions using one of the three basic motions for hands and feet. Each combined arm and leg motion creates a new position. The positions are useful when constructing a chant or cheer. Try it for yourself!

Below is a suggested motion drill for precision practice.

Motion Drill

Step One: Practice each arm motion beginning with your hands on your hips. Use your shoulder muscles to move your arms sharply. Say each step aloud and pause between each step. Carefully analyze each position for correctness.

Step Two: Practice each arm motion and experiment with various feet positions. Stop between each position to analyze form and technique.

Common Errors

Proper form and stance are crucial for developing unity. Listed are common mistakes to avoid during tryouts or as a participating squad member.

Avoid:
Eyes and chin pointed at the ground
Limp wrists and ankles.
Slouched posture
Fly away or uneven arms
Misdirected fist circles

Review each step in front of a mirror and check to see if you are executing the positions correctly. Being careful to master proper placement, run through each position step-by-step. If you practice using correct technique, you'll have an easier time grasping new combined material.

★ VOICE CONTROL

To assure the crowd follows your lead, practice good diction by opening your mouth as you enunciate each word. Avoid using words in your cheers that run together like "push 'em," "we're," or "you'll" but instead pronounce distinct words your audience can follow and understand. For example, "Push them back, Tigers." Test your enunciation during yell practice by using the two vertical fingers between your teeth rule. Tighten your stomach muscles and speak loudly. Support your voice with your diaphragm and stomach muscles. Can you feel your diaphragm pushing against your ribs just below your breast bone? With practiced diaphragm support, you can amplify your voice and project your words. Also exercise your throat. It may seem silly at first, but I know of many cheerleaders who have damaged or lost their voices by not preparing their voice.

Condition your throat muscles for the harsh activity it will perform. Proper voice control will assure your effectiveness and prevent vocal nodes that damage your voice permanently. Incorporate a vocal drill into your warm up for practice and performances. When available, take advantage of megaphones or microphones. They are an excellent choice when exercising authority and will save your voice in the long run.

Be sure to use your diaphragm and speak clearly as you over-emphasize each word. To assist you in your efforts, try performing this vocal exercise during your workout warm up session.

Vocal Drill Warm Up

Hum a low monotone for 60 seconds with diaphragm tightened support
Chant "Go Tigers Go" in a low, soft voice for 60 seconds
Chant "Fight Tigers Fight" in a medium voice for 30 seconds

★STARTING POSITION

Both chants and cheers begin with a starting position. You may decide to start with hands on hips or hands close at your side. Here is an example of a starting pose.

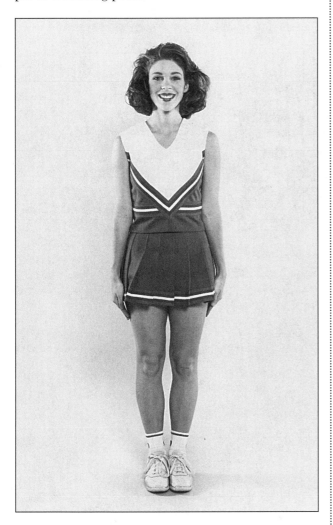

Sample Chant

The following chant will show you how arm and leg motions correspond with words. Read through my learning tips before you begin practicing on your own.

Once you have successfully mastered the sample chant, you will be ready to begin developing them on your own. There are important methods to keep in mind before constructing a chant found on page 70.

LEARNING TIPS:
Start by studying each picture for technique of arm, hand, leg, and foot position. Next, attempt the positions in each picture. After you have learned the first position, add the word to it. Now, you are ready to go on to the next step. Repeat the directions, and then go back and perform the two together. Learn the rest of the positions the same way. After you learn the position and word, repeat it from the beginning of the chant. This process will help you memorize the material you've just learned. Once you feel comfortable about the chant, test yourself using the Learning Visualization Formula.

The Learning Visualization Formula works like this:

LEARNING VISUALIZATION FORMULA

Part I
Sit in a chair and close your eyes.
Visualize the chant thoroughly and pay close attention to what your arms, legs and hands are doing.

Part II
Open your eyes, stand up and go over the part(s) you are forgetting.
Smile enthusiastically. If you practice smiling every time, you'll begin to do it automatically.

As a mental run through, the visualization formula is ideal for testing memory, but don't forget to ask for a live audience when practicing. Ask a family member or a few friends to watch you. You're more likely to make a mistake when people are watching. It's a great way to combat nervousness.

CHANT **Hold That Line**

Hold   That   Line

Sample Cheer

The following is a basic cheer for the beginner to intermediate. Apply the same learning tips from chants to your cheers.

CHEER **Go Fighting Cougars**

GO   FIGHTING   COUGARS

(PAUSE)

R

H

S

(CLAP)

BEAT

THOSE

BEARS

(PAUSE)

WIN

TO-NIGHT!

METHODS FOR CHANTING AND CHEERING

Use proper voice control.

Let your enthusiasm shine on your face and in your voice.

Keep arm motions simple enough for the audience to follow easily.

Perform specific chants to fit the game situation.

Diversify generic chants.

Once on the cheerleading squad, teach your school the chants at the pep or spirit rallies so they will be familiar with them when your squad calls for them.

Use these important methods to help you organize different chants and cheers in your game plan to fit a variety of game situations. Review the arm and leg motions in this chapter. Decide which motions you would like to use or modify. Then, add them to pre-selected words, developing each position step-by-step. To construct your own chants and cheers, try out some of the yells listed at the end of this chapter.

Formations

Patterns and formations are an active part of cheerleading. The audience is more likely to respond and stay focused if they see changing formations. Incorporate several formations into your cheers, such as diagonals, "T" positions, staggered or diverse lines and circles.

Organize your rehearsal time to learn at least one chant or one cheer per day and incorporate formations in your cheers. Rehearse a good repertoire to perform on quick notice. Construct the words to your own cheers by taking a few minutes while you prepare your next practice schedule. Check out a rhyming dictionary at your school's library. Match up action words or phrases. Make an old cheer catchy with a new phrase. You'll be surprised at how easy it is to change just a few sentences of an old cheer. Fresh chants and cheers will always bring your crowd to life.

Sample Chants and Cheers:

Abbreviations:

Clap-C

Pause-P

Stomp-S

Repeated letter indicates to do more than one time. (Example: CCC= Clap three times)

All Caps indicate emphasis on words. (Example: Get THAT ball = Emphasis on the word "that.")

Here are some sample chants for you to learn or use for practice

Chants

FOOTBALL:

Stand Up
Big Blue
That is right
Stand up team, Fight, Fight, Fight

Extra, Extra
Extra, Extra
We have might
We are Number 1
We are out of sight!

Block That Kick
Block that kick Bob Cats
BLOCK (P) THAT–KICK

Block It
Block it HEY
Block it
Every way to stop it

Take That Ball
Take THAT ball back
Hey Hey
Yeah take it!

First and Ten
First and ten Bears
Do it again
We said (repeat)

Six Points
Six points
Six points
We want (CCC)
Six points

Get It
We want it
You can do it
Get another Touchdown

Move em Back
Move them back
Down the Field
Move them back (SSC)

HEY HEY
HEY HEY
HO HO
Take that ball away

Defense
DE-FENSE
(CC) Defense
Push them back . . .
    DEFENSE!

Watch Out
Watch out Bears
The clock has begun
Gonna move that ball
We are number one!

D-I-S
Definite—Infinite—Spirit
Let's Yell

Evidence
(P) audience
There is evidence
Our offense
Is magnificent

Double Quick
Our Vikes are double quick
Come on Vikings
BLOCK THAT KICK!

We Want Six
We want six points
What do we want?(PP)
A TOUCHDOWN!

Fight
Go green
Go white
Go Go FIGHT!

G-O
Go
G-O
Go Bobcats Go

We Got the Ball
We got it
Run it
We got the ball
Go! (CC)

Do It Again
Do it again
Do it again
We want another (PP) 1st and
    10!

BASKETBALL:

Through the Net
Put it Through
Through the Net
Shoot that ball for two!

The Hoop
Who wants the hoop?
We got the hoop
We got it
Two points!

Win
Big Red
Big White
Shoot the ball, Win To-Night

Basket
Basket (C) Basket (C)
Slam it through for Two

SCORE
S-C-O-R-E
Score (C) Score (C)
Score (C) Rebels Score (C)

Hoop It
Hoop it (C)
Hoop it (C)
Come on Cats Score(CCC)

WRESTLING:

Pin
Pin (CC)
For a win (SSS)

Mighty Quick
You ARE mighty quick
Pin him
Make him stick!

Take Down

Yell Take down, TAKE
     DOWN
Yell Mat, MAT
Take down lay him flat

On The Mat

On the mat (C)
Lay him flat (CC)

Take Down

Take him down
Make him fall
Take Down

Stick

Pin him down
Roll him over
Make him stick

Cheers

FOOTBALL:

YELL

Yell for our colors
RED and WHITE (C)
Yell For Team Spirit(C)
Victory To-Night!

Go, Fight, Win

Go, Fight, Win
Never give in
GOooooo Hornets
Fight To Win!

Go-Win-Fight

Go-Win-Fight
Go tigers fight
Fight tigers win
Win tigers go
Go-Fight-Win Tigers
Win Tonight

Can not Be Beat

Two-Four-Six-Eight
We have the team(PP)
that can not (PC) be beat.
C-O-U-G-A-R-S
COUGARS . . . Can not be
     Beat!

Action

Action
Action
Our team (PC)
Yells (P) Action (P)
A-C-T (CCC)
I-O-N (SSS)
ACTION!

Welcome

Wel-come Raiders
How Do You Do?
We are glad you are here
So we can welcome you
Welcome Raiders Welcome!

Go Cats Go

Go Cats go
Blue and white
Yell Fight Cats Fight
All Right!

Hey

V-I-C-T-O-R-Y
We will tell you why
We are great
Hey, Hey
Without debate!

Hula

Hula, Hula, Hula, Har
Our team is bad
They're running hard
Hula, Hula, Hula, Hey
Move over Eagles . . . We're
     here (P) to stay!

Fired Up

Our Bears (C) are fired up
Yell Crowd (C) get fired up
Yell Red, Red
Yell White, White
We are fired up!

It is Time

It is time
To show YOUR moves
Come on Cats YOU can
     groove
It is time to score and shout
We can win with out a doubt

Go Fighting Bears

Go fighting Bears (P)
D-H-S
Beat those Bulls (C)
Win
TO-NIGHT!

Look Out

Up the field
A-cross the goal
Our teams a-fire
Watch (P) them go (CC)
They are fighting
strong(PP)
They are tough to Beat

Look out Horns . . . Take a Seat!

We all are here (CPC)
To have (P) some fun
Just one winner (C)
Our team is
The one!

We Have the Power

We have the power
Our (SS) power (S) is hot
(CC)
Gonna use our power
To Stay On TOP!

Go

Go Green
Go White
Go Eagles
Fight, Fight, Fight!

Awesome

We are A
We are Awesome
We are B
We are Bad
We be awesome, We be bad
That be US!

Boom Boom

Boom Boom
(SSS)Hey Hey
(SCS)Hear your(C) mighty
    spirit
Gold and White
Hear it (P) To-Day!

BASKETBALL:

Can not Be Beat

We are the best without defeat
We have the team
Who Can't Be BEAT!
Let's Go
We can't be beat, (P) Let's go!

Yell

Yell B-A-S, B-A-S
Yell K-E-T, K-E-T
Yell Basket Ball, Basketball

Shoot For Two

Hey Panthers
Put it through
Slam it quick
Shoot for two

Step Aside

Step aside get ready (C)
Let the game begin (C)
We have the power
To Win!

Ready

Our Tiger team is ready (C)
Ready to play (C)
Yell for our Tigers(PC)
To win THIS GAME!

Time

Time to fight
Yell today
Time to fight
Win, All Right!

Word

Say word . . . (PPP)
The word is out
We are victory bound
It's time to shout

S-H-O-U-T
Say the word (CCC) Shout!

Check Us Out

Check us out
We have the team
We are dribbling fast
We have speed.
CHECK
US
OUT!

Fight, Fight, Fight

Go Green, Green
Go White, White
Green and White
Fight, Fight, Fight!

Shoot Mighty Hornets

Shoot mighty Hornets
(C) In the hoop
The best
Is coming
Shoot for a hoop!

That Basket

That basket is hot
Our team is too
Go Eagles
Shoot for two.

Dunk

Hey Gold
Hey Black
Dunk THAT ball
Two points, All Right!

The Game

Basketball (P) is the game
Yell Blue and White(CCC)
Blue and White
Start the game

Shout for Teamwork

Shout for teamwork
Do not (P) give in
Move that ball
Hoop a basket
WIN!

WRESTLING:

Hey Crowd

Hey crowd stand up (C)
Our Vikings are on Top (C)
We have the pin
To Win This game
Stand up, Win!

He's Our Man

Number 7 he is our man
Give "CHARLES"
A great big hand (S-C-SS)
(S-C) ALL RIGHT!

Fight To Win

Fight to Win (P)
Get on top (P)
Strive for a pin(PP)
Fight to Win!

Roll Him

Roll (P) him
Move (P) him
Pin him flat
Come on' crowd (C)
Yell for (PP) the mat!

★CHAPTER 9★

JUMPS, STUNTS AND PYRAMIDS

I will never forget cheerleading camp when I saw my first pyramid. The older cheerleaders dismounted one by one from the top in symmetrical fashion. It took my breath away. They made it all look so easy. The talented display of jumps, stunts and pyramids kept me spellbound.

For modern cheerleaders, stunts and jumps are an expected part of their routine and training. Even if you are not experienced in this area, you can learn to perform many of these maneuvers if you work hard, practice and use sensible safety precautions. Although I thought it would be impossible, I learned to do a pyramid and many other jumps and stunts. You can too.

★STARTING UP

You should always warm up your body thoroughly before attempting any jumps or stunts. Slow stretching and limbering exercises are a must so that your muscles are prepared for stress and hard work. If you try to practice without warming up

properly, you will either injure yourself or wind up walking like Frankenstein because you'll be so sore.

When you practice stunts and jumps you should always have spotting assistance to avoid injuries. The spotter will assist in the stunt through the dismount, cushioning any falls by protecting your head and torso area. If you are practicing a pyramid, there should be one spotter for every person elevated in a stunt. The spotter should position him or herself about two feet away to the back or side of the base person and extend his or her arms up toward the elevated person.

Jumps, stunts and pyramids should all be practiced with caution and always on mats. Practice on a mat that is large enough to provide all stunters and spotters with adequate space.

★JUMPS

Jumps are eye-catching moves that display your individual talent. Getting noticed at tryouts is more than half the battle for making the squad. It is a necessity to acquire a variety of jumps for your repertoire so you will be able to hold the interest of the crowd. Review the spotting methods listed in chapter 6 for start-up procedures. Prepare yourself for jumps with this jumping drill.

Jump Drill

Purpose: To achieve greater height and increase timing coordination.

Directions: Jump rope for 3–5 minutes in tuck position, bringing your knees close into your chest. Unlike normal rope jumping, this style will require you to jump on a mat or padded surface to prevent shin splints.

Hints: Keep your back straight and push off the ground with the balls of your feet.

Once you feel confident with your jump height and form, you may progress to the next step. Start with the jump preparation or "prep step." Prep steps help wind up your body for the jump. Preps are characterized by the amount of time and movement needed before executing the jump.

There are several different preps for jumping. The dagger prep is a clean-looking precision style prep that most cheerleaders prefer. Position yourself properly by keeping your back straight, holding your head up, and focusing ahead. Your prep step, if performed properly, will place you in the position to achieve the highest looking jump. After mastering the prep step, incorporate a jump. Start with the basic tuck and progress in order of difficulty, attempting the hardest jump last. Your arm and shoulder motions are essential to gaining momentum, height and proper form. For maximum lift in the jump, coordinate upper body technique with timing.

The Prep

Dagger

Begin with arms in front as if holding daggers.

Tip up on toes then down to a knee bend.

Jump upward and lift your legs into your jump.

Land with feet together. Reach down placing fist slightly below knees as shown.

Stand up in ready position.

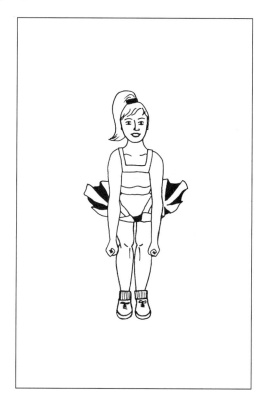

Jumps

Tuck

Keeping knees tightly together, pull your knees up and into your chest. Keep your toes pointed.

Banana

Reach arms up by ears and arch body back as pictured. Keep your legs straight and point your toes.

Spread Eagle

Straddle legs out to side; keep knees forward and point your toes.

"C"

Face side and kick legs back, to make an arc. Hold your head up.

Double Hook

Keeping torso straight, bring knees and legs up as pictured.

Russian (Toe-Touch Variation)

Keeping torso up, bring legs up and turn out; circle arms down as pictured. You can perform the basic toe-touch by stopping your arms horizontally and reaching for the inside arches.

Side Hurdler

Kick leg out to side as pictured. Bend other leg and keep knee up.

Front Hurdler

Kick front leg up to chest, bend back leg as pictured and reach arms to toes.

Split

Kick legs out one in front of the other, sitting into split position in the air.

Double Nine

Keeping head up, kick straight leg out in front and bend the other in a "nine," positioning your arms the same way.

Pike

Kick legs up parallel to the ground. Keep head up and point your toes.

Here are some key points to remember when practicing jumps:

Experiment with different arm motions.

Keep your head upright and look upward with chin up.

Point your toes and land on both feet at the same time.

Practice each jump with a spotter until you master each one successfully.

Keep your back straight during the jump and bring your legs up to your arms. Be careful not to move your arms down to your legs; it can cause you to lean forward, making your jump appear lower.

★PARTNER STUNTS

Thrilling to watch, partner stunts add diversity to the sidelines and are the ultimate crowd pleasers. Learning partner stunts requires concentration and proper technique. They require at least two persons to perform: (1) "the base" or bottom person and (2) "the mounter," the top person or "climber." Learn partner stunts in order of difficulty, with the hardest and highest learned last.

Concentration and timing are crucial when performing partner stunts. The first crucial element in partner stunts is learning how to mount another person without hurting them. Both base and mounter must work together to make the stunt work and look smooth. Many squads add variety to stunts by performing them in groups or contagions. The crowd will always be entertained with the most simple maneuvers, but the challenge is to keep them entertained with a variety of different stunts.

(Beginner–Intermediate)

PARTNER STUNTS

Pony Mount

Starting Position: Sit

Base: Stand with feet shoulder width apart, bend forward and place hands above knees. Your back should be in a rigid table top position.
Mounter: Place one hand on base's shoulder and other hand on lower back as pictured.

Sit

Base: Remain in position.
Mounter: Push off the floor and support your weight as you hop up. Sit upright, tuck your feet in close to the base, and point your toes. To pose, you may twist as pictured or remain forward.

Kneel

Base: Remain in position.
Mounter: Push off the floor and support your weight as you hop up to kneeling position. To pose, twist to side or remain forward.

Stand

Base: Remain in position.
Mounter: Push hard off the floor and support your weight as you prop up into a kneeling position. Place feet one at a time on base's lower back, release hands and stand up.

Side Sit

Base: Stand in a side lunge position; square hips to the front.
Mounter: Place shin up high on base's thigh.

Base: Hold mounter in, tightly around waist.
Mounter: Bring other leg in, sitting on the base.

Dismount:
Base: Remain still in position until mounter returns safely to floor.
Mounter: Reverse steps; brings legs to floor, one at a time.

L-Stand

Base: Stand in a side lunge position; square hips to the front; secure mounter in tightly, holding above the knee.

Mounter: Rest hands on base's shoulders, place foot high onto the base's upper thigh.

Dismount:

Base: Assist mounter in landing; catch at waist.

Mounter: Bring leg over front, raise arms up and step off in front of base.

Base: Hold mounter in tightly; reach for the ankles and lock arm straight.

Mounter: Push off ground; balance weight and tighten body while lifting leg out.

Side Thigh Stand
Heel Stretch (With spotter)

Base: Stand in a side lunge position, square hips to the front, holding above the knee. Prepare to cup mounter's inside foot.

Mounter: Rest hands on base's shoulders, place foot high onto the base's upper thigh; push hard off ground, placing other leg on thigh to arrive at a complete standing position. Hold position until stabilized.

Dismount:

Base: Assist mounter in landing, catching around mounter's waist.

Mounter: Bring leg back into stag position followed by standing. Step off the front.

Base: Remain in position and continue to hold mounter in, tightly.

Mounter: First stag outside leg, hold heel and stretch out leg as pictured.

Shoulder Sit

Base: Stand in a side lunge position; square hips to the front and hold above mounter's knee.

Mounter: Rest hands on base's shoulders, place foot onto the base's upper thigh.

Base: Step up to standing position and hold mounter above the knees.

Mounter: Push hard off ground. Place leg over shoulder followed by standing leg. Tuck feet behind base's lower back.

Dismount:

Base: Carefully bring arms under mounter's legs one at a time. Grab hands and quickly shrug shoulders upward to assist mounter in the landing.

Mounter: Hold hands with base and jump off the back. Land with feet together.

Shoulder Stand

Base: Stand in side lunge position; square hips to the front and reach arms upward.
Mounter: Hold hands with base, place foot onto the base's upper thigh.

Base: Arms should remain rigid, holding hands in position. When mounter places foot on shoulder, move to standing position.
Mounter: Push hard off ground putting weight on your arms; softly step up one foot at a time onto base's shoulders.

Base: Release hands one at a time and place behind mounter's calves. Pull downward to secure mounter in place.
Mounter: Stand up; tighten body in place to balance.

Dismount:
Base: Assist mounter in landing, catching around the waist.
Mounter: Step off the front, lifting arms over head for landing.

(Intermediate–Advanced)

DOUBLE BASE STUNTS WITH SPOTTER

Thigh Stand

Bases: Stand in opposing side lunge positions; square hips to the front.

Mounter: Rest hands on bases' shoulders, place one foot high onto the bases' upper thigh as pictured.

Dismount:

Bases: Stand up in straddle; assist mounter in landing, holding one hand and each catching under the arm.

Mounter: Step off the front for landing; raise arms out in horizontal *T*.

Bases: Remain standing in opposing side lunge positions. Place inside arm above mounter's knee.

Mounter: Push hard off ground, step up with other foot as pictured. Release hands from bases' shoulders to stand.

Shoulder Stand

Bases: Stand in opposing side lunge positions; square hips to the front. Reach outside arms upward; hold above mounter's knee.

Mounter: Hold hands with bases, place left foot high onto the left base's inside upper thigh.

Bases: Remain rigid holding hands in position.

Mounter: Continue to hold hands. Push hard off ground; step up and place other foot on right base's shoulder.

Bases: When mounter places foot on left base's shoulder, stand in upright position. At the same time, place inside hand behind mounter's calves, pulling downward to secure in place. Release outside hands.

Mounter: Stand and tighten body, balancing on bases' shoulders.

Dismount:

Bases: Keep arms rigid. Cradle catch by turning inside to each other with feet shoulder width apart. Reach arms out straight alternating arms between each other. Use your legs to support your weight. Catch mounter under arms and legs.

Mounter: Quickly lift up and off bases' shoulders; extend arms out to horizontal *T*, pike at waist and hug both bases for the catch.

Double Base Extension

Base: Turn into each other; bend and use your leg muscles for support. Cup your hands.

Mounter: (First practice placing each foot on bases' palms one at a time.)

Next, place both hand on bases' shoulders and jump up, placing both feet on bases' cupped palms. Press down keeping weight on your arms as you jump up.

Spotter: Place hands on mounter's waist and assist with mount.

Bases: Cup hands around each foot; together, lift up mounter to shoulder height.

Mounter: Take hands off bases' shoulders to stand.

Spotter: Continue to support mounter by holding around the ankles for support.

Bases: Hold feet firmly and dip together. Lift mounter up; keep mounter's feet shoulder width apart. Keep lock arms straight and rigid.

Mounter: Tighten body and balance in position; display any arm motion.

Spotter: Release waist; place hands on legs for balance and assistance

Dismount:

Bases: Facing each other, release for cradle catch. Extend arms out and bend at the waist. Use your legs to support the catch.

Mounter: Position feet toward the front, pike at waist and hug both bases for cradle catch.

Extension Tips:

Base:

Keep body still and square hips and torso to audience.

Concentrate on timing for each step.

Quickly turn in to catch mounter for the landing.

Mounter:

Push off ground.

Pull up tight and balance on bases.

Concentrate on pulling up with your chest and shoulders.

Check that bases are ready before you dismount.

★ PYRAMIDS

Pyramids are partner stunts linked creatively. They require at least three people or more to build. They are built from a combination of partner stunt formations with each squad member having an individual responsibility in the total formation. Pyramids use basic partner stunt techniques for climbing, mounting and dismounting procedures. You must be attentive. Pyramids don't just require greater concentration than a single stunt; they require your utmost concentration to prevent any unexpected falls. All those involved should know exactly what their responsibility is in performing the stunt or pyramid. Everyone must hold their own weight and never push or shove the others. One slight tug can cause immediate disaster and endanger the other participants. Pyramids are always the biggest

attention-getters at the games and are great for ending cheers or taking squad photographs. Many squads build them into cheers for variety. Use your creativity to safely build pyramids suitable to your squad. Even the simplest stunts work well in a pyramid.

Pyramid Building Tips:
  Keep your head up and maintain eye contact with your audience.
  Work together; concentrate on balancing your own weight.
  Distribute your weight evenly on the base or bases.
  Use your peripheral vision to watch the timing of the other stunters.
  Select a pyramid "buzz" word to unlink if anyone feels unstable.

★CHAPTER 10★

GYMNASTICS

Gymnastics have fascinated crowds for thousands of years. Performed in Greece as far back as 600 B.C., gymnastics were first employed as athletic training to develop the muscles of ancient Olympians. Later, gymnastics became a part of warrior training to prepare men for battle. Gymnastics did not come into its own art form as we know it today until the early 1800s. German schools adopted the philosophical ideas of Adolph Spiess, a German gymnast, in an effort to start an intensive school gymnastics curriculum. European immigration initiated school gymnastics development in the United States, beginning with Harvard University.[1]

It is not known who first introduced gymnastics to cheerleading, but early cheerleading documentation reveals the captivating thigh pitches and dive roles to mark the important beginning of gymnastics in cheerleading as we know it today. Though dive roles and thigh pitches have now been declared illegal by the National Federation of State High Schools Associations (NFSHSA), gymnastics continue to play an increasingly active part in cheerleading.

Just how important are gymnastics to cheerleading? "Gymnastics are an integral part of cheerleading," says Ann Upchurch, member of the NFSHSA Spirit and Rules Committee. "Cheerleading is easily accomplished without gymnastics, but there is no denying that gymnastics incorporated with cheerleading is very effective." Cheerleaders with gymnastics expertise have no problem pumping adrenaline into the audience. Gymnastics can be performed before, during and after cheers and pom routines.

When Should I Start?

Gymnastic skills are a combination of willpower, speed, strength, flexibility and timing. Learning gymnastics cannot be accomplished overnight. To master advanced moves requires much training, even years of study. Some gymnastics stunts may come easy, while others may be more difficult and require much more strength.

Strengthening for gymnastics takes time, so it's best to begin training early, if possible, before your teen years.

You can certainly still learn and practice some gymnastics as an adolescent and adult. Just remember, it is a long learning process and you must remain patient with yourself while acquiring the necessary new skills.

If you give yourself the leeway to learn gradually, you can concentrate on perfecting technique and form. Gymnastics can be a lot of fun for the beginner. Even beginning stunts look spectacular if performed creatively.

Where to Get Instruction

Seek professional instruction if you decide to advance beyond basic movement stunts. There are preparatory classes for all pre-adult age groups. Some gymnastics centers offer technique classes for all age groups. Scope out several gymnastics centers *before* you make a decision. There are basic issues to be aware of when planning for instruction.

If you are serious about gymnastics, here are some hints on how to select an instructor.

Seek a certified coach or knowledgeable
  trainer.
Review past experience of instructor(s) and
  inquire about up-to-date standards.
Inspect learning location for mats and proper
  spotting equipment.
Ask to view learning aids and teaching tools.
Observe class training program for your partic-
  ular ability level.
Inquire about emergency procedures.

Most schools offer gymnastics in their curriculum within their athletic or physical education departments. Your instructor should bring experience, guidance and enthusiasm to each training session. You will bring willingness, determination and commitment.

It is important to communicate with your instructor if you don't understand something you've been taught. It is your body and you are ultimately responsible for its care and well-being. Your coach is your ally; the more you ask the more you will learn. Cooperating together, you'll build a strong, well disciplined program. Whether you decide to take instruction from a private gymnastics club, community classes or the YWCA/YMCA, your gymnastics training is a great asset worth pursuing diligently!

What to Wear

There is no need to go for the latest in gymnastic fashion clothes. Be sensible and choose clothing that is functional for vigorous workout activity. Avoid clothing that restricts full body movement. A sweat suit is helpful when warming up, but it is too heavy for tumbling. It is best to wear a leotard when training for gymnastics, yet many find gym shorts and a tucked in T-shirt work well also. Remember to buy a good sports bra to wear underneath your clothing. Other than eye wear, refrain from wearing any form of jewelry, as it can hinder your performance. Wear your hair pulled back in a bun or tight pony tail so it won't get in your face or get stepped on during a move. Knee and elbow pads are a great precautionary measure, but should never take the place of a spotter as you learn a new move.

Prerequisite Exercises

Many believe that having strength and flexibility exempts them from any prerequisite training. Athletic ability will automatically prepare them for all desired gymnastic moves, right? Wrong. Even athletic people must work at working out. Prerequisite exercises involve the building of critical muscle groups to accomplish gymnastics.

There are three main training components:

Warming up, working out and cooling down. For an advantageous workout, your body must first be conditioned for the activity to follow. A cool down works the same way; it prepares you to return to your normal day-to-day activity. The warm up and cool down process are the most critical elements in a safe prerequisite training program.

★WARMING UP

Warming up prepares your muscles and allows your body to move more freely. I strongly recommend limbering the entire body before starting any strenuous gymnastic moves. Unfortunately, many beginners don't know which exercises are most beneficial. As one cheerleader put it, "I know to warm-up, but which exercises are most helpful for gymnastics?"

Warm-ups include a variety of circulatory movements. For example, a five-minute jog in place increases endurance and circulation. Your body will be ready for stretching once you increase your blood flow. Review Chapter Six for conditioning exercises. Begin with your largest muscle groups and gradually work towards the smaller muscles. Avoid jerking during stretch time, and try not to bounce when in a stretch position. The Bridge exercise (see below) is an important example of gymnastics stretching.

Maximize your warm-up by incorporating movements you regularly use the most in gymnastics. Continue your warm-up until you feel a light sweat. Begin your workout after you are completely loosened up. For power, select and perform a few recommended power exercises described in Chapter Six. The bridge, below, is great for stretching the back and strengthening your shoulders.

The Bridge

Instructions: Lie on back with knees bent and feet flat on floor. Bring arms over head and lay palms flat on floor by ears, pointing fingertips towards feet. Use legs to lift hips, followed by chest; lock arms straight and keep head back and stretch torso. Hold for 10 seconds.

★GYMNASTICS THREE-PART WARM-UP

1. Enhance Blood Supply Start with 5 minute run around room or jog in place. While running, spring jump into the air.

2. Begin Stretching
- Start with point-flex exercises for legs and feet. Sit with legs straight in front; keep back straight, point feet and bend forward, placing your chest at your knees. Open to straddle position, point toes and bend over to the right side. Repeat to center and left side. Repeat entire sequence with flexed feet.

- Proceed to back, stomach and trunk. Stand up. Start with hip, trunk and chest rotations to loosen joints. Next, kneel on mat with legs slightly apart, arch your back and reach back with arms. Then, rest your buttocks on your feet, lean body forward stretching arms and return to kneeling position. Lay flat on back, cross arms over chest and pull forward to knees. Rest chest on knees. Finally, proceed with Bridge exercises (see p. 94). Repeat sequence several times.
- Standing, windmill arms up over head and down by side. Repeat in opposite direction. Circle wrists; tighten into fists and release. In front of you, place both palms together as if praying then turn hands away from you and point fingertips to ground.
- Relax neck and tilt head forward. Slowly roll head around, starting to side, then to other side. Repeat in opposite direction.

3. Incorporate Movement Drills Stand with feet together; tuck jump to straddle or second position. Repeat 10 times. Be sure to land on the balls of your feet first. Next, raise right knee to chest; return to standing position. Repeat several times, alternating legs. Next, keeping leg straight, lift right leg up to waist or eye level and hold 30–45 seconds. Step forward and repeat. In both exercises, keep back straight and balance on left leg. You are now ready to start your workout.

★ COOLING DOWN

Cooling down is just as important as your warm up. Your goal in a cool down is to gradually lower your heart rate by decreasing physical activity. The decline helps your muscles return to a normalized state. Spend at least 10–15 minutes on the cool-down process. You may use some of the same exercises used for warming up.

★ SAFETY

Safety is an integral part of your gymnastics training program. Learning gymnastics often brings bumps and bruises. You need to be aware of your surroundings and keep your hands dry, as they tend to slip when stunting. Always practice on mats and with a qualified spotting partner. For complete safety guidelines refer to Chapter Seven.

Spotting

While you will be able to perform some gymnastic stunts without assistance, safety spotting is an essential procedure whenever learning a new stunt. It assists you in attempting a stunt through its full range of motion without getting injured. Spotting may appear simple to oversee, but there are certain techniques a spotter can learn to become more effective. As a beginner, it is wise to make a habit of learning both spotting and performing procedures. Effective spotting will enable you to assist others who are at your same level and make you a valuable asset to the squad. Read each of the following descriptions below to help you determine the appropriateness of each spotting level.

Level I—Assistance spotting involves hands to body contact from beginning to the end of each stunt. With hands to body contact, the spotter assures the movement is safely executed when the stunt is first attempted.

Level II—When available, harness spotting is the ultimate in learning advanced maneuvers. Only use the harness belt under the supervision of a qualified trainer.

Level II and III—Non-assistance spotting involves assistance readiness while a stunt is being executed. Only after assistance spotting has helped guide you to several properly executed stunts are you ready to attempt a stunt without physical—hands to body—contact.

All spotters should be alert and, preferably,

physically strong. The spotter is responsible for breaking any hard falls resulting from improper execution of the stunt. To avoid potential injury, conduct spotting on a mat.

First Aid

If you are training at home, remember to keep a first aid kit and a phone nearby for emergencies. It's always a good idea to keep your physician's phone number handy. Place a first aid manual near your practice area. First aid manuals are inexpensive and available from the Red Cross. Do *not* attempt to train for gymnastics when you are alone.

★ MOVEMENTS

When you isolate the movement of one part of your body, it directly prompts another part of your body to move. Movements are affected by proper stance and correct balance of your center of gravity. Your center of gravity is characterized by an invisible vertical line separating your body's left side from the right. Attention to balance will enable you to pick up new movements more rapidly.

To help you get started, follow this progressional movement plan. Each movement is listed in the order of difficulty. Beginning and intermediate levels are considered *slow tumbling* moves. The advanced moves are sometimes referred to as *power tumbling* because of the amount of power and strength it takes to perform rapidly. Do *not* attempt new or advanced moves without a qualified spotter or certified gymnastics trainer present. Failure to follow this advice could result in physical injury. Master each new movement *before* attempting a newer one. Once you have mastered a few, you can begin performing them in multiple series and sequence combinations. Be creative; the simple moves are great for ending cheers on the sidelines. Good luck!

Progressional Movement Plan

Here is a sampling of some of the movements you can use.

	Gymnastic Movements	Sequence Combinations
BEGINNER	Splits: Right, left and center Rolls: Forward, side, backward Backbend: Backbend, Backbend-kick over Handstand: Handstand, Handstand forward roll Limbers: Front, back	Walking splits Roll-split, Back roll-handstand Handstand knee-sit
INTERMEDIATE	Cartwheel Walkovers: Front, back Back walkover-split Tinsica: Tinsica—tuck forward roll-split Round off	Cartwheel-tuck forward roll Front walkover-tuck split Round off-back handspring
ADVANCED	Handsprings: Front, back Aerial cartwheel Aerial walkover Front tuck Standing back tuck	Forward roll-back handspring Front handspring-aerial cartwheel

The goal of your progressional plan is to start slowly and concentrate on developing proper technique. Your gymnastics coach will tell you when you are ready to advance to a more difficult move.

BEGINNER

Splits

Starting Position

Right Split

Left Split

Instructions: Bend down and place palms flat on floor. Hop into a split position by placing your front hamstring against the floor. Keep your back knee towards the front in line with both legs. Point your toes.

INTERMEDIATE (WITH SPOTTING ASSISTANCE)

Right Cartwheel

Instructions: Face body in direction of stunt. Stretch arms straight out in front of you. Keep right toe pointed and reach to ground. Place right palm down to ground in front and in line with right foot. At the same time, lift left leg up and follow in line with left in front of right palm. Center weight as legs are in air. Facing left direction, step with left foot toe to heel, followed by right foot.

Backbend

Instructions: Stand in upright position. Reach arm up and back . Lift chin back to spot floor. Hold in position. Use stomach muscles to pull up, followed by chest.

Back Walkover

Instructions: Stand tall and straight. Place all weight on back leg; keeping front leg straight and point toe. Extend arms up and reach back. Place hands on floor and lock arms in place. Keeping legs straight, lead with front leg, allowing back to follow through the line of movement. Place front foot flat on ground and briefly balance on leg as you come up to shift weight on to back leg.

Back Limber

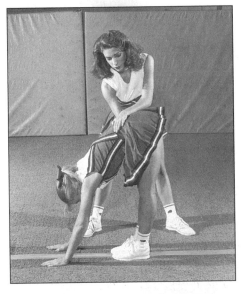

Stretch up and back, keep head back and spot. Starting with stomach and hips, pull up into handstand. Place front leg down to floor from toe to flat position; follow with back leg into a straight, upright stance.

ADVANCED STUNTS
Please seek qualified trainer for these gymnastics moves.

Front Handspring

Back Handspring

★ GYMNASTICS CHEERS

Now that you know the basics, the trick is to incorporate gymnastics into your own cheers and sidelines.

Yell and Fight

Gymnastics Cheers con't.

Stand

Stand Up Crowd, Yell and Fight

Up Crowd

Yell and

Fight (pause)

Our Bears are Hot

Our Bears

Are

Hot (clap)

Go Red

and (pause)

**Go Red
and White!**

White!

Learning Tips:

Observe motions for correct arm positions, foot placements and stance.

Polish for limp wrists, drooping arms, slouched shoulders and imprecise transitions.

Pay particularly close attention to the steps before and after the stunt.

Practice smiling.

Combine gymnastic stunts for individual or team use. Master any move before incorporating it into a cheer or dance routine. Most cheerleaders come up with two or three different moves they can substitute in place of a stunt. Try it, and notice for yourself the variety it adds to the yells and the improvement it makes in your ability to create.

★ GYMNASTICS FOR COMPETITION

Especially effective at special events and cheer competitions, gymnastics launch the audience into flying suspense and leave them craving more. Gymnastics are a powerful motivational tool to use on fans when they appear restless. How important are they from a team competition standpoint? Here are answers to several important gymnastics questions commonly asked by cheerleading squad members.

Are gymnastics required for competition?

No. Although most championship squads incorporate gymnastics extensively in their performances, many squads do not. Championships start at division or preliminary levels where the best squad(s) advance to the next higher level until the winner(s) are announced.

Are gymnastics good scoring insurance?

Power gymnastics (advanced stunts in multiple series) are helpful and show skill. Slow tumbling is not recommended at the competition level. Depending upon the competition, tumbling can be judged as a part of "cheering skills" or "gymnastics skills." Ask for a score sheet and information on competition guidelines. If performed incorrectly, or if timing is off, gymnastics could penalize your overall execution score.

When can gymnastics cause problems?

Problems can arise in a number of different ways when competing. Improper safety procedures are a roulette game that invites injury. Your squad could be disqualified from competition if proper safety procedures are not followed. While safety guidelines vary between each cheerleading association that conducts a competition, the NFSHSA has standardized guidelines every high school squad member should obey.

Gymnastics ability is an important asset in getting you noticed at tryouts. It might be just the edge you need to make the squad or the advantage your squad needs to win a competition. Gymnastics training is the best way to improve coordination and flexibility. What was great training for Olympians of ancient Greece is equally excellent training for you as a cheerleader today.

---

[1] B. Sunds and M. Conklin, *Everybody's Gymnastic Book* (New York: Charles Scribner's Sons, 1984).

★CHAPTER 11★

DANCE

ancing has entertained the human soul in every society since the Stone Age and has held prominent roles in religion, war and entertainment. The word "dance" is derived from the German word *danson*, which means "to stretch".[1] Dancing allows us to act out our feelings and emotions as we stretch ourselves beyond ordinary body movements. It's no surprise that dancing has become an increasing attraction on the sidelines, thus making it a common requirement for cheerleader tryouts.

★DANCE IN CHEERLEADING

Dance is integrated into cheerleading through flashy, dynamic choreography performed with excitement and enthusiasm. Sideline dance routines involve precise, extended and sometimes exaggerated motions that the crowd can see from a distance. The actual distance is a determining factor in the selection of dance steps, props and other key elements of routines. Pompons and other functional props are excellent visual aids to incite audience appreciation of every move.

Dance routines are typically performed during official time-outs, the fight song, pep rallies and spirit events. Like cheers, they need more time and audience attention to be effective.

Rhythm Analysis

If you want to learn to dance in a manner other than the freestyle swaying and gyrating you might do at a dance or a party, it might be a good idea to take some lessons. If you want to start on your own, you need to begin by understanding some of the basics of dance. The first thing you need to learn about is rhythm. Rhythmic beats are the soul of dance movement. Understanding rhythm is important to cheerleading dance because you are dancing with a team. Although there is room for creative expression, you will be somewhat limited by specifically choreographed movements. If you do not know how to keep to a beat you could easily throw everyone else off track. And coaches know a squad will only be as good as its weakest member. Don't let that be you.

To understand beats, tap on the table lightly with a pencil. Count the beats first in fours, then in groups of eight. Then just listen to yourself continue to tap evenly. Your mind will naturally try to group the taps into a specific number of beats which repeats itself. In music terms, rhythm is carried over into beats per measure.

The measure in music is the grouping of beats that repeat. For example, 1-2-3-4, 1-2-3-4 and so on.

The tempo is measured and characterized by the number of beats per minute. Dance steps will be counted in sets of 8 counts. Count 1 through 8 four times slowly without music. Now count it again at a faster pace. Now walk counting those beats and hop on four and eight. Try to feel the rhythm of the beats. Highly sophisticated rhythms will have irregular or syncopated rest patterns in between counts, making them more difficult but more interesting to count. The short rests in between counts may be counted as "and" or "and-a."

Examples:
I. 1 and 2, 3 and 4, 5 and 6, 7 and 8
II. 1, 2, 3 and-a 4, 5, 6, 7 and-a 8

Count the first example four times without stopping. Stand up and walk: on the even counts, accent your steps by stepping heavier and turn your head to the right. You may add a few arm motions to certain beats if you wish. Can you sense the rhythm? Your sense of rhythm represents what is commonly referred to as *kinesthetic awareness*. The fundamentals of good movement and proper form are important aspects of the awareness that you will acquire as you develop as a dancer.

There are really only four fundamental movements in dance:

Strong-precise: sharp and crisp movements
Gentle-light: flowing, graceful movements
Large-big: exaggerated movements
Small-tiny: intricate movements

Dance combines several movements to create a certain style. You can incorporate movements together in front of a mirror to broaden your development.

Style

There are many different styles of dance. Style refers to the overall thematic presentation of a movement or to one's own personal expression. In general, most of today's show dancing integrates overall theme presentation and individual style. Styles most common to cheerleading include: Traditional Pompon, Hip-Hop, Funk, Jazz, Novelty and High Kick. A routine can incorporate more than one style when you combine steps that are rhythmically compatible.

★ LET'S GET STARTED

When starting dance, wear clothing that fits comfortably and enables each movement with a minimum of distractions. For beginners, solid leotards and tights are most helpful when concentrating on postural lines. Conditioning is just as important for developing your dance skills as it is for your general cheerleading skills. Never begin dance training without a proper warm-up, even if you are only "marking" a few steps. The following is a suggested preparatory warm-up for establishing good technique.

Preparatory Warm-Up

WARM UP STRETCHES
(Use exercises illustrated in Chapter 6)

- Head to Toe Rotations
- Chest to Knees
- Leg
- Hip Flexor
- Straddle Point Flex Series
- Straddle Leg Lifts
- Stretch Splits
- Back Arch
- Heel Stretch (not pictured)

MOVEMENT TECHNIQUES

(Concentrate on proper placement)

1. Arm Punches (Punch to all angles)

2. Straddle Jumps (See chapter 6)

3. Plié-Relevé Stand with feet shoulder-width apart. First bend knees and tuck your fanny under. Then straighten legs, press up arches and heels, and balance on your toes. Correct posture is important for maintaining good balance. Hold for 4 counts and return heels back to the floor. Repeat several times.

4. Isolations *Head*—Keeping body still, stand up tall with feet shoulder width apart. Slowly move head side to side and backwards and forwards. Repeat 8 times.

Shoulders—Stand with feet shoulder width apart. Keeping right arm straight and head forward, slowly lift shoulder up. Release and lift other shoulder. Repeat 8 times.

Rib Cage—Keeping body still, stand with feet shoulder width apart and swing upper chest to the right then swing to the left, being careful not to swing hips. Repeat 8 times.

Hips—Stand in medium straddle position. Keeping torso straight to front, swing hips side to side. Repeat 8 times.

5. Kick Step Stand with feet together. Take one step with right foot and, keeping toes pointed, kick left leg forward. Place left foot to the ground and kick with right. Repeat several times, gradually picking up the pace.

6. Include across the floor basics: leaps, turns, layouts, splits and high kicks. It is helpful to include steps in your warm up similar to those in your performance routines to loosen joints. Be sure to cool down after every workout.

Preparatory Basics

Preparatory dance basics develop and improve our skills, locomotor movement, memory readiness and balance. Mastering free and proper movement through skillful control of the body's invisible center line advances your dance level instantly. Without exception, poor posture affects execution of movement and will lead to injury. To be sure that you are holding your weight proportionally, stand in front of a mirror with your feet slightly apart. Check to see if your back is straight (arms hanging evenly on each side), hips are square to the front and knees are in line with your ankles. Pull shoulders back slightly, level arms and tuck your fanny under. Concentrate on pulling up from the spine and pelvis.

Before you attempt to learn the outlined dance routine, it is important for you to understand the basic skills in relation to movement. The following are fundamental step skills. Read through each movement definition and practice in front of a large mirror.

FUNDAMENTAL STEP SKILLS:

Walk—A shift of weight or "step" from one foot to another while maintaining contact with floor.

Run—A shift of weight from one foot to the other at an accelerated speed with a brief loss of contact with the floor.

Leap—A shift of weight from one foot to the other while reaching for height or distance.

Hop—Similar to the leap, except weight remains on the same foot during landing.

Skip—A hop with small scoot forward before transferring weight.

Jump—A shift of weight from one foot to both feet or both feet to both feet.

Prance—Similar to pedaling a bicycle, shifting weight from one foot to the other while keeping the toes in contact with the floor.

Vary these skills by changing the direction of

the step. For example, a walk to the side creates a "Grapevine" step. Take time to experiment with each step by performing it to the front, back and to the side. To broaden your understanding, practice each step individually, then combine those steps in various ways until you understand their place in movement. For example: Run Run Leap Step Step Jump Hop Step.

Dance routines include a number of technical skills. They display difficulty and include splits, kicks, turns, layouts, leaps, jumps and gymnastics stunts. Practice your right, left and Chinese splits. Start your kicks to the front at 1/4 height and proceed to waist level, eye level, as high as possible. Kick diagonally, to the side and back. For steadiness, practice turns, leaps, jumps and gymnastics at one end of the room and work your way to the other side. The pirouette turn and back layout are two common dance skills for you to add to your repertoire.

Pirouette Turn

Note: This turn is performed in two counts.

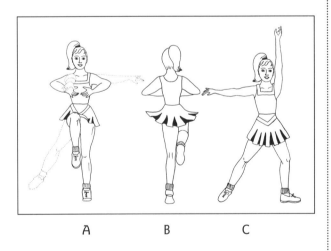

A   B   C

Count 1: (a) Lifting up onto left toe, bring right leg into left, placing the arch by knee cap. Spot to the audience while turning.

(b) Master half turn to the back before attempting full turn.

Count 2: (c) End the turn facing the audience.

Back Layout

Count 1: Step out with arms across chest.

Count 2: Kick other leg out, swing arms out into high "V," arch back and support weight with ground leg.

Count 3: Return kicking leg to ground and lift up body to repeat step with other leg.

★ KEY DANCE ELEMENTS

It is just as important to learn how to improve a dance as it is to perform one. Dance elements give routines pizzazz, ease transitions and are pleasing to the eye. They include the use of isolations, level changes, grouping, pick-ups, contagions, patterns, lines and repetition. Each element plays an integral part in an audience-pleasing routine.

1. Isolations—Confined movement of a certain part of the body. These moves usually catch the viewers off guard and generate a positive response.

2. Repetition—A combination of steps applied over. It is more effective to perform repetitious sets during the chorus of the music. When the chorus repeats, the combination repeats. Repetition works quite well for the sidelines, because the audience will be able to anticipate the movement and can perform simple arm motions along with the squad.

Repetition is a great way to involve the audience in your fight song routine, and you'll get a kick out of watching them!

3. Level Changes—The rising and bending of steps. Level changes are creative visual effects that keep the routine different even when the same step is repeated.

4. Grouping—A movement that is broken into several smaller groups. Each group performs in unison a single step or series of steps. After completion, the group holds the counts while the other groups continue to perform. The steps for the other two groups may be the same or completely different. A group holds until it is their turn to perform again. For example, for two sets of eight counts, group one can perform counts 1 through 4 and hold 5, 6, 7, 8, 1, 2, 3, 4. Group two holds count 1–4, performs counts 5 through 8 and holds counts 1, 2, 3, 4. Group three performs the second set of 1 through 4 counts, and all three groups join in together to perform counts 5 through 8.

```
1           1           2           2

      1                       2
                  3
            3           3
                  3
```

5. Pick-ups–When the leading group starts, rather than holding while others perform, they continue performing until they "pick up" all the groups.

6. Contagion–Often called a "ripple," this step is performed from one direction to another creating a domino effect. Contagions are excellent for pompon routines.

7. Lines–The rows in dance. Single, straight lines are the basic for all squads on the sidelines.

Lines should always be straight for the audience to take notice. Vary lines by staggering or create special patterns to give the routine depth. Lines create highly visible effects and are easy for squad members to perform.

8. Patterns–More commonly referred to as "formations" and made of lines of dancers that create a shape. They add an exciting element to your routines and cheers. There are six basic patterns: vertical and horizontal lines, angles, diamonds, triangles and circles. These patterns are the basics for making other formations. Modify patterns to spell out letters and words. Apply them to any routine or cheer.

Dance elements create the variety and continuity needed to make even a simple routine more interesting to watch. Now that you understand the basics, let's get started with a basic dance routine. Perform it with or without pompons. Begin by reading the directions for each step first, then follow the picture for each count provided. Give yourself some time to learn. Be patient with yourself as you practice each step.

★BASIC DANCE

Beginner (20 Counts)

Count 1: Stand with feet together, arms across chest.

Count 2: Jump out to straddle; swing arms down and out to low V.

Count 3: Invert left leg, raise heel off ground and swing left arm to right low diagonal parallel with right, turn head to diagonal.

Count 4: Raise left arm half up, fist by shoulder.

Count 5: Return head to audience, unfold left arm out. Arms will be in a diagonal.

Count 6: Jump, feet together; pull arms in tightly to body with hands in daggers.

Count 7: High kick right leg; reach arms up.

Count 8: Bring right leg to ground while twisting to the left side. Arms will be in diagonal with the left arm high and the right arm low.

Count 1: Jump to center, feet together, hands by hips.

Count 2: Twist to right side, arms in low "V."

Count 3: Twist slightly to invert right leg up, keeping the knee down and toe pointed; box arms up.

Count 4: High kick to right diagonal, bring right arm up by ear, and left arm out to side by left diagonal.

Count 5: Step down from high kick, keeping legs straight and left toe pointed with heel off ground. Bend right arm behind head; bringing left arm across to right side. Hold count 6.

Count 7: Turn to the right to face the back

wall. Bring left arm up and right arm out to side. Hold count 8.

Count 1: Turn to the right to face audience, squat and place palm onto floor. Hold count 2.

Count 3: Extend legs to right split.

Count 4: Bring arms to high V.

★ POINTERS

Avoid trying to grasp all the material the first time. Instead concentrate on technique and establishing good form.

Pay special attention to the detail of the arms, hands and torso before adding the feet positions. Watch for "flying" arms, limp wrists and pointed toes.

Count each sequence in your head, but avoid counting out loud with your mouth.

Be aware of overall movement and timing; concentrate on smoothness.

As you are finishing a step, begin thinking of the next step .

Dance lightly on your feet, and watch your individual spacing.

Keep your head up and focus on eye-contact with the audience.

Concentrate on stage presence, project a spirited image and vary your smile.

Clean and polish each step. Ask for your family or friends to give you some pointers.

★POLISHING

All routines should go through a cleaning cycle to help eliminate careless technical mistakes like misalignment and sickled (relaxed) arms and legs. Your routines should always be neat, clean and free of memory mistakes, all of which take away from the desired creation of the dance. Correct mistakes more easily by practicing in front of a mirror. Mirrors help identify weak arm positions, bad posture, hesitations and rough transitions. Concentrate on perfecting the first set of eight counts before you move on to the next set. When you have completed a 32 count combination, stop and review from the beginning. Repeat this procedure until you have polished the entire dance. Once you have completed each sequence, practice the complete routine 5–10 times from memory—without mistakes. Be aware that corrections can take hours but the investment will be worth it!

One more thing: have fun. Your joy will shine through during performance time if you practice having a good time while learning.

★GROUP PRACTICE

Unless you are receiving private instruction, it is rare you will ever learn a dance by yourself. Here are a few simple practice guidelines to apply when working as a team.

Rotate lines when learning and correcting routines. This will give everyone a fair chance to see the front one teaching.

Review your routine daily with music.

Practice each 8 count of the routine slowly without music.

Polish in front of a mirror and practice with enthusiasm .

Take turns watching and giving constructive criticism.

Practice full out every time. Don't hold back

for the performance or you may find you do not have anything better.

★HOW TO CHOREOGRAPH YOUR OWN ROUTINES

We should all learn the basics for composition. This talent does not come naturally to everyone, but anyone can learn to do it if she really works at it. Often professionals are sought to choreograph special routines, but choreography can be expensive and not every squad has the resources for such luxuries. Begin choreographing the routines that will help your squad by applying the basic skills and key transitions of movement. Choreography is a skill that is fairly easy to learn, and once you have it, everyone will turn to you for your expertise! So, let's get a head start in three short steps.

1. Determine the style.

2. Select your music.

3. Decide on which key elements to incorporate.

The most important parts of your routine are the beginning and ending. These are the parts the audience remembers the most because they usually include steps that are more dramatic than the dance itself. That does *not* mean that the middle of the routine isn't important. The middle must have high energy moves to keep the interest going. It must have moves that build towards a dramatic ending. A good analogy to choreography is a mystery movie. A mystery movie gradually provides suspenseful clues of what is to come. Finally, the movie peaks by giving a surprise ending. Your routine must follow a suspenseful and surprisingly dramatic finale. Anyone can make up a dance, but suspense is the *real* secret to choreography!

FIVE METHODS OF BASIC CHOREOGRAPHY:

1. **Creation**—Tackling each step from scratch, using your own creative imagination.

2. **Visualization**—Imagining a step in your head, then recounting what you've seen.

3. **Improvisation**—Spontaneous dancing to music, then focusing on the steps you like.

4. **Repetition**—Using a sequence of sets more than one time in a routine.

5. **Variation**—Using sets of the same routine or another routine by altering the arms, feet or counts.

By altering a sequence of sets, you can use several of these methods to choreograph. You can even use the variation method to change certain sets in the chorus for a completely new routine.

For best results, select music that has the energy level and style you desire, along with a comfortable tempo. For greater difficulty, choreograph movements to the short rests between beats. Once you choreograph a routine, perform it with different music for a different look.

WHERE TO GO FOR HELP

Dancing is one of the hardest of movement skills because it requires technical, memory and comprehensive ability. Don't wait until tryouts to decide you need extra help. Immediately begin taking classes at your school, community center or a private studio. Be sure to visit a few reputable dance studios that offer specialized pompon and dance classes. If you cannot locate a class, inquire about the possibility for private instruction. Also contact a nearby college or university squad and ask if they have a cheerleader or pom dance member who would like a part-time job instructing dance.

---

[1] Arnold L. Haskell, *The Wonderful World of Dance* (New York: Garden City, 1960).

PART V

WINNING WHEN IT REALLY COUNTS

What people see in you will influence them far more than what you can ever tell them. For me, starting out on the right foot was essential to establish me as a top competitor. Great skills are wonderful, but it's not everything if you can't uphold all of the forgotten skills that go along with the cheerleader title. These next few chapters concentrate specifically on the total candidate and how you can influence both your teammates and those who will judge you at tryouts. Your skills of winning when it really counts will put you over the top when the competition is fierce. These chapters will teach you how to get the most out of your position, and all your endeavors. Now turn the page and let's put you on that winning track to success.

★CHAPTER 12★

FIRST IMPRESSIONS: YOUR APPEARANCE

Are you a diamond in the rough? Diamonds don't start as perfectly symmetrical stones. They must be cut, shaped and polished outside before they are ready to catch the light that seems to radiate from their inner beauty. It is through the tedious work of a disciplined master that the diamond's inner brilliance is unveiled. Only then does the diamond become an object of impeccable beauty. You have so much more potential than a diamond, don't you? Of course you have! You have much to look forward to because, as with many other things, your appearance is one thing you can constantly improve upon.

People notice you by the way you look, act and talk. Your appearance is important every time you leave the house, go to school or attend important game events. It's that first impression that determines whether they like what they see and will want to know you better. At tryouts, judges do not always have time to get to know what great people we are, so they must rely upon observing your total appearance. It's sometimes what they

see that will determine how they judge us. Just keep in mind that it's your inside that determines what your outside looks like. First, you must believe in yourself and that positive change is possible. This chapter will concentrate specifically on your appearance as other people view you.

The first thing to look at are your inner qualities. Think of someone you admire and respect. What is it about that person that makes you like them? Those qualities are probably deeper than meets the eye. It is not uncommon to admire others for their strengths especially where we feel some frailty or insecurity. But don't become too preoccupied with the greatness of other people. Concentrate on the traits that make *you* special. We each have specific characteristics that make us unique and likable. On the same note, we also have certain quirks about ourselves that are just plain irritating.

You are unique because there is no other person in the world just like you—and there never will be. Spend some time to relish your inner qualities. For starters, ask yourself a few questions such as "What do I like most about myself?" Your answers should provide a clear understanding of whether or not you have a good self-image. If you see the positive in yourself, there will be no limits to your potential. When you take a good look at yourself in the mirror, you'll eventually come to fully appreciate the truly terrific person within. Now, isn't *that* wonderful? That's because when you discover your inner beauty, it will be easier to come to grips with your objective flaws. Instead of fretting over a bad haircut or concentrating on the blemishes on your face, you can look at yourself as a wonderful work in progress.

If you unconditionally like and accept yourself for who you are on the inside, you will have no trouble taking in the constructive criticism about your outside.

If you work on your attitude you will find it easier to gain a spot on the cheerleading squad and much more pleasant once you get there. People who have a negative self-image often make it difficult for other people to like them. If you are unhappy, you may be ill-tempered and cranky. Think about the constant *complainers*. Complainers are usually that way because they are frustrated about something that affects them directly. Their unhappiness is so apparent; it's difficult for others to like and accept them because they are unpleasant to be around.

That is not to say that you can't have occasional bad hair days. But if you have a chronic problem with negativity you might want to ask yourself if cheerleading is really right for you.

Happy people glow from the inside. This is an inner beauty you can't buy at the cosmetic counter.

The important aspects of your outside appearance that relate directly to your potential as a cheerleader fall into two categories: grooming and etiquette.

Basic grooming includes the way we reveal our physical features that make us attractive.

Etiquette capitalizes on that factor through our conduct and performance. Both grooming and etiquette encourage physical and behavioral improvement. Each reflects the way we feel about ourselves. With only a few changes, you can make a big difference in the way people notice you. It won't cost much more than your time and patience. Let's shape up our appearance with a few helpful tips.

★ GROOMING

Your outer appearance is important because it's the first thing people see when they meet you. You can maximize the way you look with just a few simple improvements. My personal philosophy is that you can never learn too much about looking and feeling good.

Posture

Good posture is a reflection of your mental state; it tells people what kind of person you are. For example, picture someone who walks into class with her head hung low and shoulders slumped over. It might appear that this person is insecure, shy or depressed. Is this the image you want to project? Probably not. When you stand up tall, keep your torso to the front, hold your head up and bring your shoulders back. It will tell others "I'm secure with myself." Try it! Stand up, straighten your back, pull your pelvis under and roll your shoulders slightly back. Now raise your head and put a smile on your face. Can you feel the difference? You can easily change your posture with a little conscious effort. Once you learn good posture, apply it to the way you stand, walk, and sit.

Standing—You must know people who stand in wide-straddle position as a habit. Picture a female cheerleader you may know at the homecoming dance. She's all dressed up, wearing a formal dress and heels, talking to her friends. Only one problem, she's standing with her legs spread wide apart. What's wrong with this picture? This stance is fairly common for cheerleaders because we become so comfortable with the position on the sidelines. The straddle stance is similar to parade rest, a military form of standing at ease. The stance was applied to cheerleading by the men. Let's not forget, cheerleading started with men and they made up the basic cheerleader stances. They were not made for women yet they have been adopted over the years. But, what's okay for the sidelines is not always lady-like off the field. Try standing with feet together or with one foot slightly turned out in front of the other.

Walking—Ever heard the expression "she walks clunky"? That saying refers to walking heavily on the feet. Walk with your toes pointed straight ahead and step from heel to toe rather than on a flat foot. Next, take medium steps instead of large, hurried steps, and don't forget your posture.

Sitting—We spend one third of our lives sitting down. There is a proper way to sit down. Pep rallies sometimes call for cheerleaders to take a seat during comedy skits or when the players are giving their motivational speeches. Proper sitting becomes more advantageous when a more formal event comes along, such as an annual cheerleading banquet or football banquet. There are three steps to sitting down. Walk toward the chair and turn around, step back until the backs of your legs to touch the front rim of the chair. Gently sit at the tip of the chair and slide back into your seat. Sit up confidently with your legs together. We all know of people who slouch over or sit with their legs apart. Some sit with their legs crossed and bounce their leg around in what appears to be uncontrollable nervousness. When sitting, keep your legs together and feet flat on the floor. You may cross your legs at the ankles if you wish. Don't fidget with your hands or crack your knuckles. Keep your hands relaxed in front of you with one hand upon each leg, or place them in a gentle clasped position.

Personal Hygiene

Bathing—Daily cleansing is necessary to keep your skin looking fresh and free of dirt. Use a mild soap on your body and try an exfoliation cream on those extra dry spots such as elbows, knees and calluses. Use a bath brush or sponge and massage your skin lightly. Use a hand towel to clean your chest, neck and face. I suggest using a delicate facial cleansing bar to help remove the dead skin. A fine, soft facial brush is helpful on pores. Be sure to tackle those hard-to-reach places such as the ears with a cotton swab, not your fingernails! Gently pat yourself dry with a towel, being careful not to rub eyes and face. Extreme rubbing can cause wrinkles and make your eyes red. Moisturize your body after bathing using a greaseless moisturizing lotion. Use more lotion in areas that are prone to chapping. Immediately after bathing apply medication to any skin conditions or rashes.

Brushing teeth—Brushing daily will help prevent tooth decay and gum disease. The secret to brushing teeth is to concentrate on each tooth individually. Place an even amount of toothpaste on your toothbrush and begin from the rear of your mouth. Gently brush back and forth until you reach the front teeth, then brush up and down. Brush each tooth and stay close to the surrounding gum, then brush around the tongue. Rinse mouth and toothbrush with cool water. Gently brush lips with a clean, soft-bristled toothbrush or sponge to remove dead skin from around your lips. Follow brushing with dental floss, beginning at the rear of the top teeth. Mouthwash and breath sprays are fine, but should never be used as a substitute for regular brushing.

Skin Care—Take care of your skin by daily cleansing, moisturizing and protecting it against the sun's ultraviolet rays. The sun dries out your skin, can cause skin disease and is believed to be a culprit in premature aging. I don't recommend sunbathing or tanning spas. Start now: protect your skin with an effective sunscreen lotion. You will need to wear the highest sun protection factor (SPF) when on the sidelines, especially during the hot months of the season.

Shaving—Wash area with moisturizing soap and lather generously before shaving to prevent razor burn. Carefully wash the razor thoroughly after each use. Control razor with caution as it will nick your skin easily.

Makeup—The time to wear makeup is a decision your parents can help you determine. Makeup should only be worn naturally, to accent your features, not change or alter them. The important point to consider before buying makeup is to wear products for your skin type. The secret to a fresh-looking face is to prepare. Wash your face thoroughly and apply a gentle moisturizer. Apply makeup starting with foundation base, followed by eye color and blush. Then, blend all lines for a natural look, dust with translucent powder followed by mascara, lipstick liner and lipstick. Remember to wash your face thoroughly before going to bed! First remove makeup with an oil-free makeup remover, being careful not to rub too hard on your eyes. Follow with a gentle cleanser, toner or astringent, and night cream. If you start early, you'll be the envy of all your friends when you're in your thirties. They'll be wondering what your secret is!

Problem Skin—Pimples and blackheads are the most common forms of problem skin. These blemishes usually occur more frequently during the adolescent years and during menstruation. Break outs are treatable and they will vanish with time. The important thing to remember is not to squeeze them. It's natural to want to force them along by popping and squeezing them free of oil. Unfortunately, squeezing causes scarring which can leave permanent, deep pits that are far worse than a few pimples. Instead, wash your face two to three times a day to relieve the excess oil. For intense cases, wash with a mild medicated soap or oil-free cleanser and apply medication after each washing. In some cases, it would be wise to see a dermatologist for a consultation.

Another common problem is athlete's foot, a fungus that is curable with medicated lotion or spray. Though not many will admit it, athlete's foot is just as common among female athletes as with males. It is characterized by itchy, scaling skin around the toes and foot. It is promoted through wetness and shower floors. Wear cotton socks; they absorb sweat better than nylon and polyester socks. Cleanse your feet two to three times daily until the symptoms disappear and apply an anti-fungal foot powder to prevent reoccurrence. Spray a strong disinfectant to the bottom of your shower daily to kill the fungus. You should notice positive results in one to four weeks.

Hair Care

Your hair is one of the first things people notice. There isn't a certain required way to wear your hair during off times. However, you will want to keep your hair neat and presentable at all times. Don't wait until class time to pull out your hair brush. It shows lack of respect for your teacher and classmates and will likely be remembered at evaluations. Go to the ladies' room during breaks and class changes to freshen up. The secret is to let people think you don't have to do anything special to look great.

Styling—Locate a stylist you can trust to help determine the style best for your face and most manageable for the activity of cheerleading. The important thing to remember about hair is that it should flatter your face and be kept neatly and away from your eyes. Try to select a style that will naturally fall into place. Seek a style that will be the least troublesome for practices, games and events. Colored and permed hair will need extra attention. Consider how a perm looks as it grows out. Once you get one, you'll have to continue or go through the bad hair spell until it grows out. If you have treated or permed hair you will want to take extra care to prevent split ends and dryness. Have your hair cut every month to keep split ends from spreading.

Shampooing—When you shampoo, measure a small amount that will cover all your hair adequately. Using your fingertips, gently massage your scalp in a small circular motion. This technique helps circulation in the scalp and stimulates hair growth. Follow with a conditioning rinse to moisturize dry and split ends, then rinse with cool water. Frequent shampooing tends to dry out the hair. Instead of daily shampooing, try rinsing with water every other day. For oily hair, wash daily. If you have dry or coarse hair, use a deeper conditioner after each shampoo.

Combing—Before brushing, gently comb through hair to remove excess tangles. Start at the tips and work your way up to the head. Be careful not to pull or yank too hard. Hair tends to stretch when it's wet and will break if it is jerked too hard. Wash your hairbrush and comb daily to remove excess hair and oil.

Blow-drying—As with many other things, blow-drying promotes hair damage and dryness. Take extra precaution to moisturize hair tips before blow-drying. For curly or fine hair, you may find blow-drying at a low temperature easier. For damaged and dry ends, use a hot oil treatment at least once per month and have the tips trimmed. When you take care of your hair it will be healthier and more manageable.

Hair Additives—Hair sprays and gels are especially effective during games and performances. They help to hold hair in place. Gels create the look of fullness and are effective for maintaining hair. To apply hair spray, mist on lightly and evenly from one direction to another. Hair spray can cause damage if it is sprayed on too heavily. The key to using grooming products is to look natural rather than "plastered." Be careful of those products with high alcohol content because they can dry out and damage hair.

Nail Care

Manicures—Long nails can be a nuisance and sometimes hazardous when cheerleading. Keep your hands and nails clean and free of dirt. After washing or bathing, gently press back cuticles. Use nail clippers to trim off dry skin. Use a buffer to smooth out ridges and sharp areas on nails, then apply a moisturizer to your hands and nails to relieve dryness. Because of the frequency of hand washing, it is especially effective to apply hand cream after each wash.

Polish—Colored polish looks best on long nails, but should never be worn on the sidelines. Apply a base coat first, followed by two color coats and a top coat to prevent chipping and fading. When chipping occurs, remove polish and reapply coats. For shorter nails, try wearing a light color or stay with clear. Clear polish is recommended for games and performances.

Nail Biting—The secret to beautiful-looking nails is keeping your nails neat, clean and manicured. How many times have you caught someone with her fingers in her mouth? How did it look? Did she appear controlled and self-confident? Certainly not! In fact, the nail chewing screamed out "I'm a nervous wreck." The best solution for nail biters is to keep a clear polish on your nails and a small nail file in your purse to make quick repairs in case you chip or break a nail. This care will help you refrain from chewing the nail down to the quick.

Deodorants

Body Deodorant—Because of the intense activity of cheerleading, a good deodorant will help eliminate those embarrassing body odors and wet spots. Anti-perspirant/deodorants help stop perspiration and wetness that cause odor. Try powders and talcs to help prevent rashes that can occur from excess moisture. Lightly dust your underclothes and socks. You will also feel drier and less self conscious.

Fragrances—Colognes and perfumes work particularly well for special occasions. They are not meant to help cover up odors, but to complement your appearance. Be careful to use only a small amount to avoid overpowering the people around you. A small dab can go a long way. It's best not to wear fragrances on the sidelines. Once mixed with perspiration, they can produce an unpleasant odor.

Wardrobe

Your wardrobe should flatter your face, figure and complexion. There is no need to buy a large wardrobe or spend money on the latest fads and fashions. The key is to dress with coordinating colors and patterns and to experiment with different accessories to create different looks. Select items that will flatter your appearance without cluttering.

Clothes—Try to refrain from wearing the same piece of clothing during any two-day period. Preselect your clothing and lay it out at night for the following day. Don't wait until the last minute, debating on what to wear. Be sure your clothing is clean, neat and pressed. Select clothes to complement your face and figure. If you are short or overweight, you should try to refrain from wearing horizontal lines and large prints; they tend to accentuate the waist and hips. Instead, wear vertical lines, small prints and darker colors. Dress appropriately for the occasion. Here is a simple rule of thumb:

Customary terms:
Casual—Shorts, jeans, slacks or skirt.
Formal—Short or Tea-length party dress
Semi-formal—Sunday best or nice slacks
Black Tie—Very formal; long party dress

Mix and match items to create a casual or formal look. The interview, if held at a time different from the tryouts, may be more formal and a dress or nice slacks would be appropriate. Protect your clothing by hanging it after use, reading the labels for washing instructions and mending hems and buttons immediately.

Shoes—Wear shoes that fit comfortably, complement your clothing and are made to last. Each pair of shoes fits differently, so it is important you buy shoes that fit snugly and have a protective arch. Select shoes that will keep your feet free from blisters and calluses.

Accessories—Accessories such as belts, scarves, ties, hats and jewelry all enhance your wardrobe. Use them to create different styles. They can make an outfit look original, unique, and even expensive on a small budget. A silk scarf worn around the neck, jewelry clips on your shoes or a scarf around your waist can add a new dimension to your wardrobe. Try it!

★ETIQUETTE

Manners

One of the most valuable things I learned while a professional cheerleader was how to employ basic manners when in public. As a cheerleader, you'll often wear the school colors. Everyone will know who you are even if you do not know them. They will look to you for leadership. Is your image the kind that others can look up to? We are expected to set a good example for others, so your manners are of consequence. We are really ambassadors of good will. Apply these simple courtesy tips when dealing with others:

Social Manners—Wear a smile on your face. Address elders as Sir or Ma'am. Be polite to others and follow the golden rule. Make a conscious effort to give greetings and apologies like "Good morning," "Thank you," "I'm sorry," and "Pardon me, please." Start questions with "May I" instead of "Can I." Be sensitive to others by avoiding slang and profanity. Acknowledge the kindness of other people. Always send a note for a gift, personal favor or letter received.

Table Manners—A common concern is "Is this my glass or yours?" or "When is it proper to start eating?" When dining outside the home, meals are usually served in courses. Your appetizer or soup is usually first, followed by your main dish, salad and desert. Your silverware is arranged from the outside in, as are your drinking glasses. Your glasses are on the right and your bread dish is on the left. Remember, on the right you drink it, on the left you eat it. Place your napkin folded across your lap and keep your arms off the table. When a meal is being served you should remain patient until everyone is served and the host or hostess begins to eat. Never slurp your drink, pick up your soup bowl to eat or sop up your food with bread. Chew your food thoroughly without opening your mouth to talk. Try to pause between bites to gently wipe your lips. If you must leave the table, quickly excuse yourself and place the napkin on the chair arm or lay folded in the seat.

Professional Manners—Act responsibly. Abide by the standards of the job. Make a habit of being punctual. Do things on your own and don't rely on others to do things for you. Make time to lend a hand to someone you know who needs assistance. When you help others, they are likely to remember when you need help.

★ANYTHING ELSE?

Don't forget the old cliché, "You never have a second chance to make a first impression".

When you have your interview for cheerleader tryouts you will be judged by your poise and how well you handle yourself.

For example, it is probably best, if you are female, not to extend your hand to the person interviewing. Proper etiquette would dictate that you wait until the hand is extended to you. Remember, cheerleaders and candidates are expected to be role models and therefore held to a higher standard.

Manners are considered so important to life as a cheerleader that courses are now being offered at cheerleading camps. So do not overlook this aspect of your preparation and training. Your manners can count highly toward your spot on the squad. It can be difficult at times to live up to the expectations of each squad, but you can do it. If you have doubts about your knowledge of what is good behavior, browse through a book on etiquette.

★CHAPTER 13★

PUBLIC SPEAKING AND COMMUNICATIONS

know what I want to say but I don't know how to say it." Have you ever noticed how some people can captivate an audience while others are ignored even though they say essentially the same thing? Have you ever stopped to wonder why? What is the magic of capturing an audience's attention? Why do some do it so naturally, while some completely bomb? The answer is in their style and comfortable use of an artful vocabulary.

Public communication involves listening, speaking and exchanging of ideas. A cheerleader must develop these skills because they are the essence of effective leadership. Aside from your involvement in the community you might be asked to address your audience through announcements, a speech or a special reading.

Communication skills are judged during tryouts as part of the overall package. If you are borderline and your communication skills are exceptional, you could realistically be pushed over the top and onto the squad. You may even be selected head cheerleader who, among other responsibilities, is the squad member spokesperson.

If you do not examine or practice your basic skills until they're needed at tryouts, it may be too late. The three most common public communications breakdowns that result from a lack of practice are stage fright, the "uhhs and ahhs" and delivery style.

★ STAGE FRIGHT

Stage fright is the most common reaction to shyness. Too often young people give in to their shyness as an excuse not to do something. That's because it is easier not to try than to risk saying something that might sound silly to others. But doing what you fear builds confidence and helps conquer shyness. Your audience is made up of people just like you. Speak to them as if you are speaking to one person; it really works. When you speak to one person rather than a large crowd, you are more likely to feel self-composed. Overcome your fears by remembering that your audience is made up of everyday people like you. Stage fright is always unexpected.

Donna describes her experience with stage fright.

Mascot tryouts were over and our big bear senior mascot just finished his last farewell with a comedy skit to *Honeycomb*. I was on next. The first of fourteen to tryout for the junior varsity squad and I knew my speech was *not* going to be as funny as his act. As I ran towards the microphone, my mind ran the other way—out the side door. Dazed and petrified, I had this uncontrollable urge to disappear. The audience was waiting for me to say something. It seemed like an hour and I kept hoping for someone to get me off the court. Uhhhh. My mouth moved but nothing came out. So many eyes were staring at me and not one person was smiling. With each passing second my chest grew heavier and heavier until I could not breathe.

If you suspect stage fright might occur, prepare a small outline to help you keep your thoughts moving. Practice reading your first sentence just before you begin to speak. Keep it in the palm of your hand, pompon, or taped to the microphone for insurance. Seeing your words will usually set your mouth in motion and prevent a complete mental meltdown in front of the entire student body. Before you realize it, you won't have time to feel intimidated; you'll be in control. Remember, conquer your fears by acting to prevent them!

If you find you are becoming tense, take a few deep breaths and talk to yourself. Talk yourself out of being frightened. The mind and body are so connected that any negative thought can trigger a physical reaction like a blank mind or frozen mouth. If you talk your mind out of having those thoughts you will head off a stress reaction before it happens.

★ THE UHH TRAP

Do you get impatient with people who don't express themselves well? All the "Umms," "Well-uhs," "Uh-huhs," "Hmms" and "You know what I'm sayings" are empty expressions. Truth is, we all say them to some degree, but it is important to jettison them from our thought patterns. Those ineffective little words tell others "I'm struggling with this, and I don't know what I'm going to say so it's not going to be important." Who wants to listen to someone who has announced to everyone what she is about to say is not going to be important? Worse, constant stammering drives the listener to *tune out* the one speaking.

Nothing is more frustrating than speaking to someone whose mind and eyes are someplace else! The mental upset of being ignored can prompt more stammering, can make you feel hostile toward your audience, and can ultimately cause a breakdown in your speaking confidence.

★ DELIVERY STYLE

Isn't it a pleasure when people speak to you in terms that you can relate to easily? That's because you and everyone else would rather listen to someone whom you perceive as caring about communicating with you. The way you deliver your message is your style. Your style, which includes your tone, is almost as important as what you say. You have your own style which will clearly emerge the more you continue to communicate in this fashion.

One day after I finished teaching a cheerleading training class, a very talented head cheerleader told me that she could never get the crowd to listen to her. She seemed irritated, so I asked her to explain her situation. She said, "I always start with 'All right, everyone do *Pump It* with us.' The crowd just sits there every time we start chanting. They just won't listen and participate."

From her authoritative tone it was apparent

the student body was not responding to what they may have felt was a demand for them to respond. I told her of a wise saying I once heard: "If the old stuff ain't working, try something new." I encouraged her to empathize with the audience, use her imagination and change her style. Crowds don't like being talked down to. They get bored with the same cheers and same methods of getting them to respond. They enjoy one-on-one treatment, the kind that evokes positive energy.

The following week, I went to see her in action. When the pep rally began, the head cheerleader backed away from the microphone to begin her yell. She shouted, "Are you ready to fight . . . Are you ready to win . . . Are you ready for Action?" The squad immediately went into the *Action* cheer and the crowd went crazy. Why do you think the crowd was responsive this week? After the pep rally I asked her about the changes she had made and this is what she said. "I decided to challenge the crowd in such a way they couldn't refuse."

A little creativity goes a long way. Challenge the audience in a personal, enticing style. If a listening audience isn't responding, try to get them to respond by communicating with them personally. At first, style changes may seem hard to make, but when you constantly work at perfecting your delivery, those adaptive changes will become just another part of your style. Good speakers can adapt and relate to an audience. And, when you take the trouble to speak to your audience's needs, they will hear your interest and respond. So, here's the key: empathize with your listeners and engage them with your message. Every audience responds to being talked to in a more personal way, particularly if they are being beckoned with a challenge.

★ TIPS TO TACKLE COMMUNICATION PROBLEMS

Work on your shyness and prepare an outline when speaking in public.

Jettison unproductive "Ums," "you knows" and slang from your speech.

Talk to the listeners empathetically and lead them to action.

Now, let's get started with some solid communication basics!

★ SEVEN STEPS TO BETTER COMMUNICATION SKILLS

1. Be prepared. Think about what you need to say ahead of time. Ummming, gum smacking, hair pulling, hand fidgeting and foot tapping are distracting. We need to remind ourselves that other people can tell when we are nervous and uncomfortable. Spend a few minutes talking in front of a mirror or to a small audience at home. It will take some serious effort to rid yourself of all the bad habits, but you can do it! Start eliminating those habits and your ability to hold the audience's attention will improve.

2. Speak clearly. Speak at a moderate speed and enunciate each syllable of each word. Pause between each point to emphasize your points. Use your diaphragm muscles as you breath and vocalize. Concentrate on the diction method you learned for chants and cheers in Chapter Eight.

3. Develop your technique. Pause before talking. This will allow you time to catch your breath, adjust your tone, and to think quickly before opening your mouth. Concentrate on being concise while engaged in conversation. Use action phrases such as "Support our team." When you speak with action words, you captivate attention rather than boring everyone to death with phrases like "Our team needs your support." Be sure to emphasize your points when you speak. Practice inflection of your voice tone on different words within a sentence. Notice how the sentence takes on new meaning with every change in tone? Tape record yourself saying sentences different ways, then go back and listen for ways to improve.

4. Strive to make yourself understood. Only you can put your vocabulary to work. This is your style of delivery. Someone else's style may work for a while but it won't be the real you, and it won't take long for people to figure out that you're not being yourself. An audience is always more willing to respond to someone who has something important to say and a distinctive way of expressing it. A good vocabulary is essential in expressing yourself. One of the best ways to foster vocabulary improvement is for you to carry a pocket synonym, antonym and word dictionary with you every time you read and study. When you hear or read a word you don't understand, look it up; then find its synonyms and look those up too. Before you know it you will have learned the meanings of ten new words and diverse ways of using them.

5. Once you have grasped a firm understanding of a word, begin using it immediately. Why will this help you? A broad and lively vocabulary can become one of your most powerful assets in capturing the attention of others. Remember, it is always a good habit to learn new words and make them a part of your working vocabulary. It's worth it, and you'll be proud of yourself for it.

6. Listen to yourself and others. Remember, one half of communication is listening to others! This takes no practice to master, only the discipline to control your tongue. Not only will you become a better listener, but you will discover people who speak especially well. Pay close attention to their phrases and word selection. Make it a point to smile or give a gentle nod to your listening party to let them know how interested you are in what they have to say.

7. When you acknowledge others as you speak, you are showing them that what they have to say is important too. Think of the last time you spoke to someone. Was that person interested in what you had to say? If not, how did that make you feel? Probably uneasy and insecure. And so remember this: whether you're speaking to one person or a thousand, it is important they all feel recognized. Believe it or not, the audience can instantly tell whether you're genuinely interested in their needs.

★LANGUAGE SKILLS

Language skills are much more important in today's world than they ever have been. Proficiency in communication will make you an extraordinary person. The first thing you can do to improve your skill is to check out a speech training book from your local library. Then consider continuing your education in speaking and in learning at least one foreign language. Informal classes are very effective and are available at most local community colleges. Why do I suggest that a cheerleader learn a foreign language? At the very least, it will broaden your horizons. In addition, the opportunities for cheerleading and instruction in foreign countries have increased dramatically in recent years.

Your communication skills will play a major factor in the lifelong achievement of your dreams. The words you select are the building blocks for improving your communication skills. Strong communication is a combination of balanced tone and creative style. Maximize your potential by improving your communication skills.

★REVIEW EXERCISES

1. Prepare a short introduction about yourself and repeat it in front of a mirror or to a family member.

2. Take two minutes to discuss why you want to be a cheerleader and discuss it with a family member.

3. Prepare a five minute oral speech regarding the experience of training to become a cheerleader and deliver it to a family member.

Use the guidelines outlined in this chapter to critique your performance on each of the exercises. Repeat the exercises for greater improvement.

★CHAPTER 14★

THE TRIUMPHANT INTERVIEW

The selection of a cheerleader can boil down to some very personal factors. If the coach interviews you for a spot on the squad but is given the impression you would be a difficult person to work with, your skills and appearance are not going to guarantee your selection. The interview is used to determine what kind of person you are as a contrast to how dynamic you might appear. It has a great deal of weight in the decision-making process, so do not ignore it as unimportant.

The reasoning is that there are many underlying traits that affect our performance besides our abilities: namely, our character. The purpose of the interview is to determine a candidate's personal attitude, standards and willingness to go the extra mile. All of these considerations enable the interviewers to determine whether you will be a team player and an asset to the squad.

Interviews are more common at the college and university level, however more and more junior and senior high schools are discovering its value. The interview may be conducted by the cheerleader coach, advisor or a panel of judges.

Because there isn't much time to get to know you personally, they seek relevant answers to how you see or envision yourself serving the squad.

This chapter is about how to portray your best qualities in those few short moments. Prepare your time wisely to convince the judges that your personal traits will be beneficial to the squad. They have a limited amount of time to decide what they like most about the individuals they interview, so your interview is a great opportunity to make up for lost points.

★ JUST WHAT ARE THEY LOOKING FOR IN THE INTERVIEW?

"Her attitude is most important. I want someone who doesn't want it all to themselves and is a good role model," says Lucy Moore, cheer coach at Rowan County High School. Cindy Tyler, coach at the College of Saint Francis, has this to say: "We try to see who the leaders are, to find out if they are flexible. We have a hard-working athletic team and a reputation to uphold. Our candidates must understand that image and not alter our reputation." Cheryl Moss, cheer coach at Mississippi Baptist College says, "We want to see how they will fit in as a squad member. We want them to be confident yet humble." Cindy Tyler agrees, "I like someone who doesn't brag."

Whether interviews are conducted by your coach, director, advisor or sponsor, they all seem to look for the same common characteristics. They all want to know five things about you:

1. Your positive philosophy
2. Clear personal goals
3. Level of commitment
4. Flexibility to adapt
5. Good people skills

The questions might be like these:

1. Philosophy—Your philosophy is your outlook on cheerleading. Why do you want to be a cheerleader? What is a cheerleader's responsibility to the school and community?

2. Goals—Your goals are what you aim to achieve personally on the squad. How can you help the cheerleaders become more effective? What personal expectations can you bring to the group?

3. Commitment—Your willingness and determination to help the squad reach it's objectives is your commitment. Remember "stickability" in Chapter One? Will you stick to the task even when the going gets tough?

4. Flexibility—Your plan of action for organizing your time to practice and attend required events, and your ability to adapt to changes. These represent your level of flexibility. How do you see yourself participating with the squad?

5. Good People Skills—Your desire to work and get along with, as well as to support, others in a team setting defines your people skills. How would you help build camaraderie? Are you the kind of friend and teammate people can look to for motivation?

To help them understand you better, perhaps you will want to share a story about yourself. Try to say it in one or two sentences. You should rehearse potential interview questions as well. Interview questions vary for each squad and are more detailed for returning squad members. Here are some examples of potential questions for you to practice with a family member or friend.

★ POSSIBLE INTERVIEW QUESTIONS

1. What are your goals in life and in school/college?
2. What do you like most about yourself?
3. What is your biggest fault?
4. How do you view your role as a cheerleader?
5. How would you describe an ideal cheerleader?
6. Who do you think is the very best candidate for cheerleader?
7. What is the biggest problem facing our school and students? How can you help?
8. How will you be an asset to the squad?
9. How can you convince me that you are a team player?
10. If you were head cheerleader, how would you resolve a conflict between squad members?

All of these questions, which in varied forms are used in the business world, are asked to find certain kinds of information. For example, Number 3—"What is your biggest fault?"—is somewhat of a trick question. If you answer with something like "I don't like to share and work with other people," you could be doomed. It is always important to answer any question in a positive manner so that it enhances your good character traits. A positive answer might be "I work too hard." It is good because it can never really be viewed as a fault to anyone interviewing you for a demanding position. Be creative with your answers.

Before your interview practice going over potential questions like these for 45 minutes each day. It is best to start at least one month before tryouts begin. You'll be much more relaxed and confident going into the interview when you have prepared yourself for the event ahead of time.

★ INTERVIEW DILEMMAS

When I conduct interviews it seems everyone seems to expound on their shortcomings but is less likely to focus on her assets. Here are the four most common interview dilemmas.

1. Responding to Negative Statements What if the interviewer makes a negative statement. For example, "I notice you've had some trouble with your grades." Are you willing to crack under pressure by taking the offense? Of course not! If you weren't eligible to try out for cheerleader last year because of bad grades, turn the situation into a positive opportunity to tell the interviewer what you have learned from the experience. Show the interviewer you can turn lemons into lemonade and can hang in there when the going gets tough.

2. Breaking through Preconceived Perceptions Regarding Past Activities "I don't want to prejudge anyone; I want everyone to have a fair chance," remarks Cindy Tyler. Let's face it, nobody is perfect and even coaches know that. We all have said or done certain things that we aren't proud of, but don't allow them to become

mental monsters. In the interview, show a good positive attitude and a willingness to work under constructive criticism. Discuss positive things that you want to achieve when given a chance. You can't convince the judge that you will be a positive asset if you dwell on the negative things about your past! Remember, if you want others to believe you've changed, you must first believe it yourself!

3. How to Tackle Controversial Issues Controversial questions are rarely asked; nevertheless, they do sometimes come up. They are usually very broadly stated, and that is the main reason they are so difficult to answer. It is always best to prepare yourself for this possible scenario rather than being caught off guard. Many times, these questions are asked just to see how you would handle yourself if put in a leadership position. The opinions of a leader are those that are valued and respected. Here is an example:

"How do you view the increased drinking age?" In this case, think deeply about what they are *really* asking. Are they really asking if alcohol is a problem for students, or whether it has a place in cheerleading?

If you don't know or don't care to answer: If you are unclear about what they are asking, simply ask the interviewer to restate the question in more specific terms. There may be times you do not wish to share your opinion or times when you feel the question has no relevance to your abilities as a cheerleader. If you still don't understand or don't care to answer, deflect the question by saying, "This has been debated for several years; it would be difficult for me to answer such a question in just a few short minutes." Never answer by shrugging your shoulders with "I don't know." You don't have to provide an answer, but keep in mind that you may miss the opportunity to state something positive as it relates to cheerleaders.

If you wish to answer: All things considered,

try to answer only if you are clear of the *intention* of the question. Keep your answer focused. Perhaps like: "Alcoholic related deaths among the teenage population are certainly of great concern but it would be difficult to answer such a question in just a few short minutes." This approach will keep your answer concise, drive away many areas for debate, and eliminate further discussion. Respond informatively rather than starting your answer with "I agree with it" or "I don't agree."

4. Protecting Private Matters There may be questions that are asked to find out how your parents will support you financially, emotionally and physically. Suppose the question is "How do your parents feel about your trying out for cheerleader?" The interviewer may want to know if your parents are excited about your trying out, if they are willing to help you get to all the required events and whether they can help finance your uniforms. It may appear trivial to some, but if your parents are in the middle of a divorce and their finances are tight, that question may appear as an invasion of privacy. In that case, you might say "It would be difficult to answer in just a few short minutes" or add "Perhaps we can discuss it after our interview." In any case, private matters should be thoroughly discussed with your parents prior to tryouts so you can deal with them head on. The important thing to remember is to be focused, honest and concise with your answer.

★TEN STEPS TO A TRIUMPHANT INTERVIEW

Now that you know the common characteristics coaches look for during the interview as well as possible interview dilemmas, apply these ten easy steps to a triumphant interview.

STEP ONE: DRESS APPROPRIATELY AND SIT UP STRAIGHT

"Posture is the first thing I notice" says Cindy Tyler. "I can usually tell what they are thinking by the way they carry themselves." No matter what age level you are, your appearance is important to your success and will say as much about you as you can say about yourself during the entire interview. Therefore, it is important to plan ahead of time and dress for the total person from head to toe. Your appearance tells the interviewer that you are responsible and mature enough to realize the importance of an interview. Be sure you, your clothing and shoes are clean and neat. The object is not to outdress everyone, but to dress responsibly. Review the appearance tips in Chapter Twelve.

STEP TWO: BE YOURSELF

One day after I judged tryouts for a professional team, the director told me "People always try to give the answers they think I want to hear. I want someone who can think for herself." It's natural to want to please someone when we want something so badly. Nevertheless, you are important and you have special talents that have brought you this far. Recognize that the interviewer is a typical person, not the master of your destiny. You are! Let your personality shine from the moment you sit down until the time you leave. Give the judges the opportunity to find out as much about you as possible.

STEP THREE: CONSIDER EACH COMPLIMENT

Compliments to the interviewer must never be dwelled upon during the interview. Too often they appear insincere, as though you are trying to buy points. On the other hand, compliments regarding the cheer program are acceptable and appreciated, as long as they apply to the questions you are answering. Knowing how to receive a compliment is just as important as knowing when to give one. Growing up, I had the hardest time receiving compliments. If someone said, "That's a pretty dress," I would say, "This dress is really old." It wasn't until I was a senior in high school that a friend embarrassed me in front of a group of people by saying "Don't give her any compliments, she doesn't accept them." I realized she was absolutely right! I thought if I thanked people for their compliments, I would appear "stuck up." Wrong! What's more, the message I was giving people was that their compliments were not appreciated. Accept compliments graciously with a simple "Thank you." Practice common courtesy and good manners throughout the interview. It shows that you are mature and considerate of others. Another point to consider: if a complement is worth giving, it's worth receiving too.

STEP FOUR: PAUSE BEFORE YOU SPEAK

Allow yourself some time to think about your answer. Don't forget, time is of the essence. If you need extra time, try restating the question as you begin to speak. For example, if you are asked, "How do you see yourself leading the squad?" Start by answering "I see myself leading the squad . . . ." Take the time to frame your answer rather than blurting out one you'll be embarrassed about later.

STEP FIVE: SPEAK POSITIVELY

Positive speaking is about turning bad into good, a negative into a positive, something sour into something sweet. It's saying something useful at every given opportunity and not allowing negativity into the interview. It's about acknowledging your accomplishments as they relate to cheerleading, without sounding too proud and overconfident. It's a difficult task to master, but you can do it! The object is to sell yourself to the person conducting the interview; but there is a fine line between positive "self-promoting" and sounding

boastful. Beware of having a boastful style that tells others a selfish, self-centered person is speaking. Cheerleading coaches and advisors know boasting spells trouble. Self-confidence entails explaining your positive areas, while indicating that there is much room for growth and improvement. It's having an air of wisdom and excitement about the future by encouraging yourself and others to seek the best.

STEP SIX: GET TO THE POINT

Do not give answers that are too long, unclear or need further explanation. Carefully word your response instead of dragging out the issue. Speak directly to the point to demonstrate your readiness. Once you do, the rest falls in place.

STEP SEVEN: PROVIDE LEADING ANSWERS

Although it cannot be helped at times, try not to answer in one word responses of "yes" or "no" or "okay" unless you are reaffirming a statement made by the interviewer in acknowledgment or agreement . Seize the opportunity to expand on something positive. For example, if the interviewer breaks the ice with "Hello, how are you today?" you might respond, "Just fine, thank you. I've been preparing for this day for a long time" rather than "Okay." The first response tells the interviewer you are excited and have been planning for cheerleader tryouts, and encourages another question such as "How long have you been preparing?" That's your chance to let them know just how dedicated you have been the past few months in training and tells the interviewer you are the kind of hardworking individual she would want on her team! I've seen too many times where young people miss out on the opportunity to give a leading response

STEP EIGHT: DON'T ANSWER A QUESTION WITH ANOTHER QUESTION

Remember who is conducting the interview. I

once asked a young lady, "How do you view teamwork?" Her answer, "Important, don't you?" I wanted her to tell me about her version of teamwork. Her version would have told me three things: (1) how important teamwork is to her; (2) how would she strive to make teamwork a success, and (3) whether she was the kind of person who would take the lead in creating teamwork. Unfortunately, in her case I didn't get to find out just how important it was to her because she was more concerned with what I thought. If you don't understand the question, you might ask, "Would you mind rephrasing that question? I am unclear about what you are asking." Try to refrain from asking questions until the appropriate time. In some cases, the interviewer will allow you to ask questions at the end of the interview. Of course, if you have prepared, you won't have any questions about the tryouts process during the interview; you will already know what is expected.

STEP NINE: AVOID TRITE ANSWERS AND EXCUSES

Trite answers and excuses take the excitement out of the interview. Dull or overused statements can lose their meaning if called on too frequently. Refrain from starting your answers with apologetic phrases such as "forgive me for saying this but . . ." and "I'm sorry but I . . . ." Apologies should never become a feature of your style, but should be reserved for when they can be sincerely given. They also call attention to circumstances that only you may be aware of. Unlike excuses, apologies are useful courtesies spoken to acknowledge an event or situation. You should also refrain from making excuses but, rather, concentrate on solutions. Excuses tell the interviewer you'll find a way to justify your failure to work hard, be punctual and act as a team player.

STEP TEN: RELAX

With all these steps to remember it may take some time to make them natural parts of your interview and conversation style. Concentrate on your posture, look interviewers in the eye and speak to the point. Try not to fidget, tap your feet, shuffle papers or clinch your fists during the interview. Remain calm and relaxed by taking several deep breaths before your interview. You can do it!

★ MORE INTERVIEW TIPS

Don't be intimidated by interviewers. For example, one director told me, "She has ten minutes to convince me she is a team player and can handle constructive criticism." Meet the very serious types with earnest, clear answers.

Do your homework and know ahead of time about the team history, the squad and the activities they actively participate in.

Tell the interviewer how long you've prepared for the event and how.

Humbly discuss why you make the best candidate.

Be truthful in your answers.

Don't speculate about the team and organization.

Concentrate on your message.

The interview is your opportunity to make up for other areas of skill or physical traits where you feel you may fall short. Interviews are your doors to opportunity; if you practice good conversational interview style, those doors will open for you. And remember, you will be interviewed at many other times in your life: for work, college, bank loans or anything you decide to undertake.

It's within your power to succeed; all you have to do is practice these steps toward improvement. Go seize your opportunity as a cheerleader candidate, and make those crucial interview moments count!

★CHAPTER 15★

THE SUCCESSFUL TRYOUT

Typically, tryouts are held in the spring, beginning with a parental or student meeting for those considering trying out. The meeting enables the coach to discuss all the responsibilities involved, pass out tryout packets and go over the tryout procedures. The graduating seniors usually will be on hand to offer assistance and to discuss their positive experiences. They will be the ones to lead the training clinic which will teach potential candidates what they need to know.

The tryout packet typically includes the eligibility guidelines, sports and appearance schedules, tryout and selection procedures and schedule, waiver forms, cheerleader agreement and a detailed cover letter to your parents explaining tryouts, rules, goals and financial obligations. Read it thoroughly to avoid asking embarrassing questions you could have answered for yourself.

★ ELIGIBILITY

Before you can participate in tryouts, you must be eligible. Why are eligibility requirements impor-

tant? The primary objective of eligibility requirements is to ensure each cheerleader maintains her status as an active role model for fellow students to follow. Inquire about cheerleader eligibility requirements as early as possible. The following is a list of universal requirements for you to consider.

1. Enrollment Requirement: You will need to find out if you must attend the school full- or half-time and if there are any residency requirements. Some schools require students to live within a twenty mile radius of the school; others require students to have been enrolled in their school for at least one year before trying out.

2. Academic Requirements: Passing grades with a C average and good academic standing are most common. However, many schools are now requiring a B average or better. Avoid being misinformed. Ask to see current scholastic guidelines for activity participation; written guidelines are updated each year. Grades must come first, so you will want to manage your study time wisely.

3. Physical Fitness Requirements: Schools must protect themselves from any possible liabilities. A current physical check up and your parents' written release should be on file with the school. You must be fit and able to adjust to non-stop cheerleading activity in conditions of extreme heat and cold.

4. Attendance Requirements: Each school has a certain number of designated games, community and special events cheerleaders must attend. There will be specific times and a certain number of days per week required for practices. Remember to glance over the official school calendar for potential conflicts with your personal schedule. Inquire about procedures for authorized changes in scheduled appearances and written rules regarding penalties for tardiness or absences.

5. Financial Requirements: There are fees for camps, specialty clinics, small social events and travel expenses to away games and cheer competition. Nearly all cheerleaders can expect to buy at least one uniform. Read carefully through the list of required finances to protect yourself against unexpected expenses.

6. Leadership Requirements: Cheerleaders must always be alert and attentive to the game and audience. Each cheerleader must be able to take it upon herself to practice, invent crowd pleasing ideas and be respectful in and out of uniform.

7. Waiver Forms: You will be given several forms to fill out. Follow the deadlines for return because there will usually be no exceptions to the rules. Handle all of your forms in strict confidence. All forms must be signed and returned by the deadlines given.

- **Parental Consent Form:** A brief letter to your parent/guardian informing them of cheerleader tryouts and asking them to grant permission for you to tryout and participate. This is a typical parental consent form:

Sample Parental Consent Form

Dear Parent/Guardian,

Please read through the packet of materials for tryouts closely with your son/daughter. This packet includes information regarding the upcoming cheerleading tryouts process, our standard rules and guidelines, and your financial responsibilities. Please return the form below to certify that you have inspected all materials.

_____ have read all information associated with the cheerleader selection and activity process and agree to allow _____ to participate as an active member of the _____ cheerleading squad at _____.

I also understand that my son/daughter is required to follow the constitution and other guidelines set forth by the cheerleading squad and will fulfill my part in seeing that such guidelines are enforced. I further understand that violations in school conduct and squad rules or failure to meet eligibility requirements, will result in immediate dismissal from the squad. I realize I will be notified in writing for violations which affect membership.

Signature _____

Date _____

- *Medical Liability Release Form*—Certifies you have been given a recent physical checkup and are free to participate in cheerleading. It authorizes medical treatment in the event of sudden injury. The Emergency ID form informs the coach and medical authorities about pertinent information regarding your health and must be filled out completely.

Sample Medical Release Form

I, _____, the Parent/Guardian of _____ hereby certify that my son/daughter has been evaluated by a family physician and is eligible to actively participate in athletic activity. I grant permission to _____ to notify medical personnel and authorize full medical treatment for any injury transpiring from his/her performance while cheerleading.

Signature_____

Date_____

Sample Emergency Identification Card

Name_____
            (Last) (First) (Middle Initial)
Address_____

_____

Zip_____Phone(Day)_____
(Evening)_____Other _____

In case of emergency, please notify: _____

_____

Relationship_____Phone _____
Allergies_____
Current Medical Conditions _____

_____

List any medications you are taking_____

_____

Personal Physician _____
Address_____
Phone_____
List all previous injuries: _____

_____

Have you ever had surgery? (Yes) ___(No) ___
For what
Condition(s)? _____

_____

_____

• *Candidate Evaluation Form*—Allows teachers to evaluate your performance in class. This form, filled out by several of your teachers, gives the coach an idea of how well you might perform in a leadership role.

Sample Candidate Evaluation Form

Your Name: _____
Teacher:_____Class:_____
Poor Average Excellent
1. Attendance: ____ ____ ____
2. Punctuality: ____ ____ ____
3. Attentiveness/Timely Assignments: ____

_____

4. Appearance: ____ ____ ____
5. Friendliness: ____ ____ ____
GeneralComments:_____

_____

_____

_____

Signature:_____
Date: _____

8. **Other Forms:**

   • *Questionnaire*—Many coaches require you to take a short sports quiz, fill out a form regarding your goals if you make the team, or ask you to write a short essay on "Why I Want to Be a Cheerleader."

   • *Cheerleader Constitution/Agreement*—The constitution sets guidelines and requirements a cheerleader must abide by. The agreement is designed to inform each cheerleader of basic goals, standards, responsibilities, procedures and requirements she must conform to during each term. Take the agreement home and review it with your parents. Make sure you go over each section in detail so that you will fully understand what is expected of you if you make the squad. Here are a few ideas of what the constitution might include:

Sample Cheerleader Constitution

I. Philosophy

The _____ cheerleaders will serve as the primary support group to lead and direct spirit for athletics, special events and activities. Members shall encourage school pride, good sportsmanship and a positive image in school activities. Education is foremost in cheerleading, and good personal conduct is not limited to the sidelines. Members will strive to project an image of high standards, morals and goals for others to follow.

II. Eligibility

1. Members must maintain at least a C average.

2. Members must remain in good school standing.

3. Members must have all required documents and forms on file.

III. Membership

1. There will be no more than _____ freshman cheerleaders, no more than _____ junior varsity cheerleaders, and no more than _____ varsity cheerleaders.

2. Alternates will not exceed _____.

3. There will be _____ manager(s). Term will begin _____ and will conclude _____.

4. Unexpected vacancies will be filled at the discretion of the coach.

IV. Responsibilities

1. A head cheerleader will be voted upon by new members at the first meeting. In the event of a tie, the coach will cast the deciding vote.

2. The selection of head cheerleader will be based on tenure, experience, outstanding leadership qualities and assertive abilities.

3. Other offices to be voted on by members include: spirit chairman and public relations chairman.

V. Attendance

1. Regular attendance at school and rehearsal is expected.

2. All cheerleaders are required to be present at all assigned games and spirit events.

3. There will be no excused absences except for illness.

4. Absences will result in the cheerleader sitting out of the following game.

5. Tardiness will not be tolerated or accepted and will be handled through disciplinary action.

6. All members must take part in all fundraising events.

VI. Conduct

1. All cheerleaders must demonstrate good sportsmanship abilities at all spirit-raising events.

2. All cheerleaders must control their behavior and follow the rules and regulations of the school and squad.

3. Each member shall follow the high standards and goals of the team.

4. Each member shall demonstrate good manners to others at all times.

5. Failure to comply with the rules and guidelines set forth by the squad will result in disciplinary action

VII. Disciplinary System

1. The Merit/Demerit Disciplinary system will enforce all good works and violations.

2. Merits account for _____ points, demerits for _____ points.

3. A written warning notice will be sent parents after receiving _____ demerits.

4. Upon receiving the _____ notice, said member will be discharged from further participation.

VIII. Appearance

1. All members must keep a clean and neat appearance.

2. There will be no jewelry worn at practice, games and events.

3. Pompons should be cleaned with a cloth and laid to dry after heavy rains.

4. Members will trim strings from pompons and fluff them before each game.

IX. Physical Requirements

1. All members must be in peak physical condition and capable of rigorous activity without danger to life.

2. All members must follow nutrition and conditioning program as set by squads.

X. Uniforms

1. Each member is responsible for maintaining all uniforms.

2. Uniforms and props must be stored properly.

3. Members will be responsible for replacement of lost or stolen items.

4. All uniforms paid for by the school must be returned not later than _____.

XI. Fees

1. Members will be responsible for paying $_____ for _____ uniform(s).

2. All members must pay for transportation fees, travel expenses, and camp and competition fees not to exceed $_____.

XII. Practice

1. Practice will not begin without the direct supervision of the coach, and a substitute will be present in the event the coach is absent.

2. All practice sessions must adhere to safety spotting rules.

3. All practices will be organized by the coach and head cheerleader.

4. All practice sessions will begin with a warm up and end with a cool down.

5. Members are expected to take learning material home to practice.

6. All members shall raise their hand to make a suggestion or ask a question and wait until the end of practice for problem discussions.

XIII. Games

1. All members are responsible for knowing all game rules and sports signals.

2. All members must welcome visiting cheerleaders and display hospitality .

3. All members will arrive at games promptly and fully dressed; then begin stretching on their own and reviewing game day material.

4. All members shall perform game day cheers in a positive manner.

XIV. Tryouts

1. Tryouts shall begin in the spring of every school year.

2. Squad selection process will be determined by: _____.

3. Judges will be selected on the basis of experience, objectivity, and knowledge.

4. Scores will be tabulated by averaging the following: _____.

5. Tryouts will begin with an opening meeting, followed by the training clinic.

6. Tryouts will consist of: _____

7. In the event of a tie, the coach will cast the deciding vote.

8. The new member announcements will be made on _____.

9. The first practice following tryouts, will involve passing out an address list, taking squad measurements and establishing season commitments.

★ ATTIRE

Always be clean, neat and pressed even when in "workout" wear. Select clothing that is loose and comfortable. Typically, shorts and a T-shirt or crop shirt are best for tryouts. Do your best to wear your school colors for the actual tryouts. Bring a warm up suit or jumper to slip over your shorts when you leave.

★ TRAINING CLINICS

Training clinics typically start at least one week before tryouts. They are a week long and last from one to two hours after school. The clinics should give you an idea of how practices are conducted. Candidates are taught by graduating senior cheerleaders. They are there to assist you with questions, watch your technique and assist with spotting. They teach cheers, chants, jumps, a dance and minor stunts. The purpose of the personal chant, cheer and dance gives them a chance to see your creative abilities. You will be responsible for creating the motions and steps for tryouts. Typically 3–5 jumps and gymnastics are sufficient. Most partner stunts are judged on how well you and your partner can perform in both base and mount positions. Bring a small tape recorder and notebook to training just in case dance notes and music are not provided. Obtain what is needed so you may practice at home. Be sure to take a notepad and pencil to record the important learning material for practice at home. Make the most of this week. Here are some suggestions to help your practice sessions run smoother:

Stand where you can see the material being taught.

Don't go home without asking questions about anything you do not fully understand.

Follow directions closely, be attentive and respectful.

Watch for technique.

If written cheers, sidelines and dance steps are not handed out after class, be sure to write the steps down on paper before you go home to practice.

★ MEMORY

Everyone learns at a different pace. Give yourself time to memorize the steps. Commit yourself to learning for the long term, which means practicing just a few minutes each day. If you don't grasp a certain step the first time, keep on working at it until it comes naturally. The best time to make mistakes is when you are learning. Here are four techniques to assist you in memorizing cheers and dance routines.

Word Association—Label each step or series of steps with a symbolic word.

Written—Write dance steps down on a sheet of note paper. Read through the steps several times.

Repetition—Physically walk through each step and repeat over and over until you master it.

Recall—A mental run-through of a series of steps. This method works great when you're in bed just before you shut your eyes to go to sleep.

Apply as many of these techniques as you need until your cheers and routine become automatic. After you feel you have mastered the steps, perform them toward a different wall in the room. The change in scenery will test your memory.

★ PRACTICING AT HOME

The week of tryouts will seem extra busy because you will be learning so much material. Organize your practice wisely by following the progression chart on the next page. This will help you pace yourself.

Follow the chart to help you assess your abilities before the tryout date. Rate your daily skills on a scale of 1–10, with ten being the best. Watch your overall score get larger as you improve!

★ ★ ★ Progression Chart ★ ★ ★	MON	TUE	WED	THURS	FRI
Jumps: (List all required)					
Tuck					
Spread Eagle					
Gymnastics: (List all required)					
Splits-Rt. Lt. Chinese					
Stunts: (List name of stunt)					
Base					
Mount					
Spotting					
Motions:					
Audition Chant					
Personal Chant					
Audition Cheer					
Personal Cheer					
Dance:					
Group Dance					
Personal Dance					

Tryout Skills Assessment

Personal Goals:

1. History (squad, sports, school) _____

2. Nutritional & Conditioning Goals _____

Required Skills:

3. Chants _____

4. Cheers _____

5. Jumps _____

6. Stunts _____

7. Tumbling _____

8. Dance _____

Evaluations:

9. Mock Interview _____

10. Essay _____

(100 Points) **Total**_____

(1–2) Poor (3–4) Fair (5–6) Average (7–8) Good
(9–10) Excellent

143

SAMPLE TRYOUT CHEER: **GO TEAM WIN**

GO

WIN

DO IT

AGAIN

GO

TEAM

WIN!

Provided is a sample tryout cheer you may use for tryouts. You may substitute the jump for any you prefer. Now let's cheer!

144

This is a sample of a score sheet a judge or panel of judges might use to evaluate your performance. It is taken into consideration with your personal interview and other factors.

Sample Score Sheet
Candidate Number_____ Judge Number_____

Chants and Cheers

	CHANT 1	CHANT 2	CHEER 1	CHEER 2
1. Voice Projection (strong and clear)	____	____	____	____
2. Appearance (clean and neat)	____	____	____	____
3. Showmanship (spirited and energetic)	____	____	____	____
4. Audience Appeal (exciting and interesting)	____	____	____	____
5. Arm Motions (sharp and polished)	____	____	____	____
6. Creativity (variety)	____	____	____	____

Dance

	DANCE 1	DANCE 2
1. Energy	____	____
2. Timing/Rhythm	____	____
3. Strong use of pompons	____	____
4. Execution (memory)	____	____
5. Technique	____	____
6. Spacing	____	____

Skills

	JUMPS	STUNTS	TUMBLING
1. Difficulty	____	____	____
2. Technique	____	____	____
3. Effectiveness	____	____	____
4. Variety	____	____	____
5. Stability	____	____	____

Evaluations

Interview _____
Essay _____
History Quiz _____
Judges Total Score _____

Average
Judges Score
Candidate Evaluation
Student Vote

★ IT'S YOUR TURN

As you prepare for your tryout, concentrate on yourself rather than on the other candidates. This means do not look at what others can or can't do. You will need to screen away negative thoughts. Sometimes there will be girls who view you as nothing else but competition. In their effort to win at all costs, they are likely to try to psych you out by attacking your confidence. A person can do that with a crossways glance at your legs as you practice your best jump. Even though you are confident your jump is good, you will be contaminated with that little bit of doubt. Do not allow it to get to you mentally. Show good sportsmanship and don't lower yourself to that level.

Keep your chin up, and do your very best. You can accomplish your dreams without having to do it at someone else's expense. Compete only against yourself and your image of triumph. I believe anyone can accomplish dreams in life if they believe in themselves.

Just remember, once you believe in yourself, you're already a winner.

Be sure to get plenty of rest the night before tryouts. Lay out your necessities in advance and glance through them twice before you leave for school. Here is a checklist and tips to get you started:

Tryout Checklist:
  Necessary forms
  Tryout clothes
  Shoes
  Music
  Extra change of clothing
  Makeup
  Hair accessories
  Deodorant
  Fingernail file
  Pencil and notebook
  Calendar
  Personal items
  Tape recorder (for backstage rehearsal time, if permitted)
  Small snack
  Other important items

Tryout Tips:
  Show excitement and enthusiasm from start to finish.
  Focus on posture, eye contact and varying your smile.
  Articulate in a clear, loud and strong voice.
  Make your motions smooth, strong and precise.
  Recover if you make a mistake.
  Concentrate on stability when performing your stunts.
  Listen carefully to the tempo.
  Take advantage of your time and the floor space provided.
  Give it everything you've got; it's the chance you've been waiting for

CONSIDER THE ALTERNATIVES

"But it's not fair." Unfortunately, not every one can make the cheerleading squad, but it doesn't mean that there was favoritism involved. In fact, complaining sounds a bit more like sour grapes. Not making the squad doesn't mean you're a bad person, or that people don't like you. Don't knock your self-confidence if you don't make it; there is always a squad in your future for next year. Now is a good time to work on the things that may have hindered you this year while they are fresh on your mind. Things always work out for the best if you remain positive. Rise above the disappointment, loss and resentment; hold your head up high and be thankful for the learning opportunity. You have truly accomplished so much, haven't you? You're in great shape now and you carry yourself with confidence. Let your worthwhile qualities shine. If you concentrate on your losses and hurts in life, you can fall prey to resentment and jealousy. Don't allow your sad disappointments consume your life and cast shadows on your future successes. Remember, things always work out for the best if you remain positive.

Suppose there's no next time for tryouts? There is always a next time when it comes to achieving your life-long dreams. Seek other ways to serve your school. First, ask the cheerleader coach if you can help the organization or how you can help raise team spirit on an individual basis. Get involved in your community, school clubs and activities. You have so many things to offer.

★CHAPTER 16★

A CHEERLEADER: SIX KEY ELEMENTS

You have made the squad! Now are you ready to discover just what is involved besides cheering at the games? One of the most meaningful aspects of cheerleading is leadership. Making a positive difference at your school by setting an example for younger students is very rewarding, but it also requires courage. Your position entrusts you with the power to positively or negatively influence others around you. All eyes at your school will judge you by the standards you keep. That doesn't mean how pretty you can be, but how genuine and kind you are among your peers, and what type of lifestyle you display for all to see. From this aspect of cheerleading, you truly get back what you put in as a friend and a class leader who sets the standard for those around you. These high expectations helped me learn to be more serious about my dreams and my life in general.

Becoming a cheerleader makes you a role model. You need not ask for that part of the job; it always comes with the uniform. Obviously drugs, alcohol and smoking have no place on a cheer-

leading squad. They hinder your health and performance. When considering the legal perspective and questionable options for behavior, ask yourself, "Are they within the law?" "Will I be glad next week that I do these things?" "Can I talk to my parents about this?" and "Can this wait?" You have a responsibility to your school, your squad and yourself to just say "No, thanks" to some who are pushing a negative lifestyle on you. You will never be sorry for rejecting destructive behavior patterns. If there is one thing to learn from reading this chapter, it is not to fall prey to the peer pressure system. Destructive behavior disintegrates your self respect, self confidence, motivation, and ambition and it's also grounds for automatic dismissal from your squad. *Remember, self respect commands respect from others.*

★SIX KEYS TO MANAGING YOUR LIFE

Cheerleading brings with it many unusual demands. Here are six key suggestions to help you manage your life successfully:

One: Time Management

How does a cheerleader fit everything into a full day? You must schedule your day so that every hour is important. Anticipate a full schedule and do not overload yourself with outside projects; an overload can encumber grades and eligibility. Your grades are most important, and establishing good grades while cheerleading is an accomplishment to be proud of. It is difficult to start these things, but once you're in the habit, life will become easier and you will have more leisure time for yourself.

1. Scheduling Purchase an inexpensive pocket weekly calendar with room to take notes for each day. Prepare your weekly "to-do" agenda and stick to it! Set a daily schedule from the time you wake up until the time you go to bed. Include study breaks, meal times, practice and games. Set your priorities by listing time-consuming activities from most important to least important. Schedule your outside activities only after you have fulfilled your commitments. Record all game, practice and special appearance dates and times and keep your calendar with you as a reminder.

2. Study Skills Designate time to study for each class and schedule it in your weekly agenda. Carry a text book with you at all times and study while on breaks, waiting around, or when on trips. You will be surprised at how many hours per week you gain with this little trick. Irrespective of your age, take a study skills course *now* to learn and apply strong study habits. You can make a big improvement in your grades and learn with more efficiency.

Ask your school librarian about study-skill courses available on videotape, or ask where you can sign up for a study skills class.

Study Hints:
Always listen in class.
Study every day without TV, telephone or other disruptions.

Study with your dictionary.
Keep up with assignments and reexamine them one week before each test.
Rewrite class notes so that you understand them completely.
Paraphrase each chapter you read into a condensed one-paragraph version.

Hints for studying for exams:
Don't wait until the day before to cram.
Apply one week of intensive study on chapters and notes for each test.
Check out library resources two weeks ahead of the test to beat the rush.
Give yourself a mini-test.
Ask your teacher if they have a sample test you can review.

Two: Yearly Objectives

Participate in outlining the squad goals and ideas for the year. Set attainable goals and make them the centerpiece of every practice session. Squad goals should cover these six key elements and must be measurable and attainable.

1. Duties Separate duties and responsibilities within the squad will assure that everyone does their part in the week-to-week demands on the squad. Different squads do it different ways, but the most common offices and responsibilities are as follows.

(a) Captain/Head Cheerleader—You must act as intermediary between the squad members and cheerleading coach. Help your coach encourage squad unity and find solutions to squad conflicts. Call group meetings, notify members of schedule changes and assist in organizing rehearsal and game day repertoire. Preach a positive, winning attitude to the group.

(b) Spirit Chairman—Organize weekly spirit events, coordinate paraphernalia, spirit sales and the display of spirit props, such as cue cards, posters and banners, for each game. Organize a spirit committee of pep club officers, drill team and pom squad members to designate comprehensive spirit duties. Meet with appropriate administrators and spirit organizations to discuss and finalize pep rally and school spirit ideas. Some squads elect two members to cochair this demanding position. Here are some school spirit ideas to get you started:

Spirit Ideas:

Select the play of the week and promote it through the use of banners and announcements.

Have a "show your spirit" theme week. For example, Monday have a '50s day, and Tuesday have a western day. Conclude the week by wearing the school colors.

Write encouragement cards or decorate the players' school lockers.

Decorate the school with spirit signs the morning of each game.

(c) Public Relations Chairman—Notifies the school office of spirit announcements; publicizes times and locations of events, rallies and bonfires; and sends press releases and photographs at least one week before important events to radio and television stations, as well as to the school and local newspapers. The following is an example of a press release:

Sample Press Release

FOR IMMEDIATE RELEASE
Contact:
[*Sponsor name*]
[*School address*]
[*School phone number*]
**Annual Christmas Food Drive
for the Needy House**
The [*name of school*] cheerleader's announce the Annual Christmas Food Drive for the needy.

Donations of canned or dry goods may be dropped off at [*location and address*] between the hours of 8:00 A.M.–4:00 P.M. All donations must be received by 4:00, Wednesday, December 20th. All donations will go to support the Needy House.

(d) Manager—Assists coach and squad with daily activities; prepares equipment set-up for practice and spirit events; prepares refreshments for breaks; and runs necessary errands. This position is often filled by a person who would love to be on the squad as an active member but, for whatever reason, is not on the squad.

2. Practice Always arrive early to warm up and review any uncertainties in technique or scheduling. Remember, everyone on the squad faces a hectic personal schedule, and no one should have to wait on you. Tardiness and unexcused absences normally will cause you to sit out one or more games. Work out technique or memory problem areas on your own time so you can come to practice prepared. Push your squad toward excellence by being attentive to instructions and making the most out of each rehearsal. Your squad's practice sessions should move the group toward the squad goals. Refrain from talk that is not relevant or constructive to the squad. Practice is not a time to express disgruntled feelings you may have toward any member or the director.

3. Teamwork Support your teammates by offering to help spot, critique and watch. Encourage friendship and discourage jealousy. Be conscious of your teammates' feelings when you give constructive criticism and respond positively when it is given to you. Work on building unity instead of fences. It only takes one person to start a chain reaction throughout the squad. Enthusiasm and a great attitude are highly contagious, and it's your duty as a team member to assist in spreading them.

4. Game Day Don't miss out on generating spirit and making new friends at optional pre-game meals and rallies. Arrive early to games, greet the visiting cheerleading squad when they arrive, and show them all the necessary dressing room facilities. Review your game day schedule and your positions along the sidelines. Follow your game day rules and show good sportsmanship by congratulating the other teams when they win.

5. Community Service Your cheerleading role does not end at school; it reaches out to the community. The squad should be actively involved in community and charity events. Here are three ways for your squad to assist your community:

> Volunteer to assist charities in raising money or donations.
> Visit a local children's home.
> Sponsor a neighborhood clean-up day.

Three: Fundraising

Why is raising money so important? Many squads raise money to buy additional uniforms, attend camps, competitions and special events. Fundraising teaches team members how difficult it is to raise the money necessary to meet the squad's financial goals. Fundraising usually begins as a mundane task, but it soon becomes a fun and exciting opportunity that builds squad togetherness and a treasure chest of memories to look back upon.

Fundraising Ideas:
> Host a bake, garage or raffle sale
> Sponsor a school dance.
> Sell gourmet food or retail items.
> Offer a cheer clinic to elementary or junior high squads.
> Host a recycling campaign.

Fundraising Tips:
> Set a personal goal and a team goal.
> Compete for a prize or award.
> Publicize event and sale items.
> State how the money will be spent.
> Approach students, local businesses, neighborhood community and family friends.

1. Events Funds raised will help pay for trips and special events. The amount will determine your budget, feasible projects and events. Squads who raise large amounts of money are able to do greater things such as make parade appearances, take trips, or participate in national camps and contests. *Great American* specializes in assisting spirit organizations with fundraising. Write for their information kit:

Great American Opportunities, Inc.
P.O. Box 305142
Nashville, Tennessee 37230
(800) 251–1542.

2. Supplies If you participate in uniform selection, order early and choose strong, comfortable and durable fabrics that are affordable and appropriate for the weather in your region. Some fabrics are more expensive to clean than others. Shop and compare for the best quality and price. Consider the cleaning bills and normal wear-and-tear the uniform will go through during the season when selecting the fabric, style and accessories. Coordinate socks, shoes, pompons and megaphones with the uniform style. Leather footwear is preferable, and most squads are now using athletic multi-training shoes. Weather gear such as jogging suits, sweaters and rain ponchos look great and come in handy throughout a long sports season. Contact one of the cheerleader supply companies listed below for a catalogue on uniforms, supplies and spirit paraphernalia.

Varsity Spirit Fashions
P.O. Box 341789
Memphis, Tennessee 38184–1789
(800) 533–8022
Items: Uniforms, pompons, shoes

U.S. Cheerleader & Sport
Specialty Co., Inc.
P.O. Box 158
Diamondale, Michigan 48821
(517) 646–9371
Items: Uniforms, pompons, shoes

Complete Sportswear Services
151 Cross Timbers
St. Charles, Missouri 63304–0421
(800) 441–0618
Items: Uniforms, pompons, shoes

Angela King Designs
285 W. Shaw, Suite 207
Fresno, California 93704
(209) 225–2412
Items: Dance wear

Cheerleader Danz Team
P.O. Box 660359
Dallas, Texas 75266–0359
(800) 527–4366
Items: Uniforms, camp wear, shoes

The Cheerleader Shoppe
5847 Ramsey Street
Fayetteville, North Carolina 28311
(919) 488–2600
Items: Casual wear

Four: Camps and Clinics

Many spirit associations host summer camps and private or seasonal clinics. They train all-girl and coed squads with new and exciting chants, cheers, dances and stunts. Instructors are highly skilled, trained and motivated individuals who provide beneficial training to new squad members. Your squad may attend a camp, clinic or both. Summarized below are some advantages of camps and private clinics.

Advantages of Summer Camp:
   Expert instruction, attention and fellowship with other cheerleaders.
   Learning the latest chants, cheers and new dance moves for the coming year.
   Helpful, constructive advice for squad development.
   Specialized captain and sponsor seminars.
   Summer competition with other teams.

Advantages of Private Clinics:
   Private instruction.
   Selected cheers, sidelines, and routines individualized to fit your squad's training needs and ability level.
   Larger amount of spirit material provided.
   Greater one-on-one treatment.
   Scheduled at your convenience.
   Designed to help you learn at your own pace.

Five: Pep Rallies

Take an active role in implementing new ideas to encourage school spirit. Create special theme ideas for homecoming and special events. First, hold a comprehensive meeting with all squad members and discuss the themes most likely to rev up the student body. Next, schedule a meeting with the proper school administrators, your coach, spirit organization leaders and band director to discuss the possibilities. Then finalize the spirit ideas, pep rally order, time schedules and clean up schedules for each rally.

Planning for your first pep rally will set a precedent for the rest of the year. Keep your pep rallies interesting by changing the format each week. Pep rallies offer an excellent opportunity to teach your student body the words to your yells and chants. Pep rallies typically last between 20 to 45 minutes; therefore, to keep your rally moving smoothly, you'll need to set time limits for each event during the rally.

Typical Pep Rally Order:
Cheerleaders give introductory chants.
Class yells begin.
Spirit yell contest between classes follow.
Band plays school fight song.
Drill or pom squad performs to fight song.
Players come out during fight song.
Squad performs a dance routine or skit show.
Cheerleaders perform cheers and teach to the audience.
Players give speeches.
Spirit stick and spirit awards for the week are awarded.
Band plays and everyone sings school song.

Rally Ideas:
Promote weekly spirit stick competition between classes.
Invite faculty to dress up like some of the players and make the audience guess who they are.
Invite senior players' mothers to the pep rally to compete for the "best cheer."
Have a sack race in which the president of each class competes.
Invite a former player to speak and promote the team.
Act out the play of the week.
Have a pie-eating contest.
Have a "Spirit Olympics."

Review skits with your coach one week before the pep rally and send a rally schedule to your school administration, band director and other necessary parties three days before the pep rally date. Work with fellow spirit organizations and your public relations chairman to promote the upcoming rally, game and events. Keep the momentum flowing by organizing game day caravans and displaying spirit signs along the highway to the games and the annual bonfire.

Six: Competition

From the local to national level, competitions make all cheerleading squads reach for perfection. Cheerleaders of all ages from all over the country are now competing for coveted titles in competitions. The phenomenon of competition is advantageous, because seeing other squads perform challenges your squad to give their personal best. Attending a competition is a great way to see how your squad stacks up against some of the best squads in the country. Contact the spirit associations listed in Appendix B for a list of dance and cheerleading camps or competitions in your area.

★ WHAT THE SIX KEYS WILL DO FOR YOU

Being a cheerleader is one of the greatest activities you can do with your life and will certainly be the among most memorable. The Six Key Elements blend together to create an unparalleled package of fun and exciting opportunities for you as a cheerleader. Jessica, from Austin, Texas, agrees:

I had never been a cheerleader, so when they called my name at tryouts I did not fully realize what was about to begin! Not long ago, I had too much time on my hands, watching television and eating junk food after school. Since becoming a cheerleader, my time has been productive; I feel like I'm doing something important for my school. I feel great, and cheerleading has had everything to do with it. This has been the best school year ever!

Like all things in life, the more you put into cheerleading the more you will love it and benefit from it. Make the most of it!

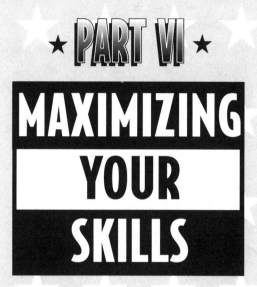

★ **PART VI** ★

MAXIMIZING YOUR SKILLS

The spirit opportunities available for your personal self-fulfillment are loaded with potential. Everything you've learned can be easily applied to other spirit-raising groups. If you think cheerleading is fun, and you want the chance to try something new, I know these next three chapters will add to the most memorable times of your life!

If you do not make it onto a cheerleading squad this year, consider some other possibilities for expressing your enthusiasm and team spirit.

★CHAPTER 17★

MASCOTS

Mascot symbols found their way onto American college campuses in the late 1800s. A unique display of homage, the school symbol soon became a standard in virtually all high schools. It wasn't long before the mascot symbols graced the uniforms of nearly every new sports team across the country. Early mascot mania ushered domesticated wild animals to the sidelines. Character mascots flourished as many schools discontinued the tradition of live animal mascots, in view of high expenses and liabilities. Recognized for their spirit-lifting performances and individualized comedy skits, character mascots became as important to the team as the symbol itself. What started with a sketch of a pen, brought to life talented and animated mascots who have leaped into their school's history and traditions. Even the Olympics have mascots these days!

Mascots today may possess a friendly, sarcastic or ferocious temperament. Their sole purpose is to generate a contagious enthusiasm for team spirit. One challenge to today's mascot is to induce a positive response from the audience when the team is struggling for a win.

A mascot at the University of North Texas describes one such experience.

It was scorching hot outside and our team was ready to raise the white flag. It was well over 100° inside the brand new, large Eppy Eagle head. Stargazed and straining to see through the tiny peep holes, I noticed the Greek section losing interest. The zany character of my secret identity kicked in to high gear. I strolled over by doing my usual *bird walk*. Covering my eyes and peaking between my wing feathers, I poked fun at them making gestures as if bored. Then I twiddled my wings and pointed towards the goal for a score. Immediately, the audience began chanting "Touchdown . . . touchdown . . . touchdown!" The audience came back to life and our team exerted harder. We won the game after all. I feel I was a part of making it happen.

People say mascots have more fun than anyone on the field. Mascots come in all shapes, sizes and personalities, but their common purpose is to add enjoyment to a game and evoke school involvement. Mascots are clever, creative and persistent. They are endlessly resourceful when it comes to generating enthusiasm. Character mascots enlighten doubtful moments of the game and, when necessary, provide comic relief for spectators. Comic relief is especially effective when certain groups within the crowd are not participating with the rest. As the team's inspired symbol, mascots are valuable in gaining control of a group that is behaving unfavorably. They use their personality to instigate positive repetitive responses from the audience by encouraging the team to try harder. Becoming a school mascot is a great alternative way to make your mark and make a difference.

★ RESPONSIBILITIES

Mascots have certain obligations they must meet. Every school has its own set of specific responsibilities and requirements it wishes to follow. All mascots have three basic responsibilities.

1. To attend all required events.

2. To ensure proper care and maintenance of the costume.

3. To promote spirit, encourage participation and give unwavering support to the school and team.

Mascots must follow these three basic responsibilities for an entire elected term. Examine each one carefully. Can you arrange transportation to attend all required events? Are you willing to keep the costume clean and neat looking? If the answers are "yes!" and you can commit yourself to number three, then you've jumped the first hurdle.

★ ELIGIBILITY

Before you can participate in tryouts, you must be eligible. Why are eligibility requirements important? The foremost purpose for having eligibility requirements is to ensure the mascot is an active role model for students to follow. It is important to ask about mascot eligibility requirements as early as possible. The following are a list of universal requirements for you to follow.

1. Enrollment Requirements: You will need to find out if you must attend the school full time and if there are any residency requirements. Some schools require students to live within a twenty mile radius of the school; others require students to have been enrolled in their school for at least one year before trying out.

2. Academic Requirements: A requirement of passing grades with a C or 2.0 grade point average in good academic standing is most common. However, many schools are now requiring a B average or better. Avoid being misinformed. Ask to see current scholastic guidelines for activity participation; written guidelines are updated each year. Grades must come first, so you will want to manage your study time wisely.

3. Physical Fitness Requirements: Schools must protect themselves from any possible liabilities. You must be fit and able to adjust to non-stop activity in high temperature conditions while on duty as a mascot. A physical check up and written release are usually requested during tryouts. But whether or not a check up is required, it is a good idea to see your doctor prior to training for this or any other kind of strenuous exercise.

4. Attendance Requirements: Each school has a certain number of designated games, community and special events they would like their mascot to attend. There will be specific times and a certain number of days per week for required practices. Remember to glance over the official school calendar for potential conflicts in your personal schedule. Inquire about procedures for authorized changes in scheduled appearances and written rules regarding penalties for tardiness or absences.

5. Leadership Requirements: Mascots must always be alert and attentive to the game and audience. The mascot must be able to take it upon their self to practice, invent crowd pleasing ideas and be respectful in and out of costume.

In preparation for your personal interview, be sure you read through each requirement at least twice and take notes so you will be ready when the time comes. Keep a qualification checklist with you when gathering answers. Your checklist will guide your efforts to overcome potential obstacles. Preparation will keep you one step in front of the others. Once you fully understand what is expected, you can add those expectations to your training goals.

★ TRAINING

Productive training begins with a list of goals. Goal setting provides a solid foundation for success. Take a few moments to review your qualification checklist. Study your strengths and weaknesses. Is there room for improvement? Absolutely! There is always room for improvement. The more you work with yourself to reach a desired outcome, the better you'll be at working with other people. If you make constant improvement on your training foundation, you'll be ready to build a strong, spirit-filled program.

Mascot training is dependent upon the traditional or desired role at your school. Special training may be needed if you are required to take part in the precision moves with the cheerleading squad. Your training program should begin with an outline of the traditional or desired role for your school. If you don't know, don't be afraid to ask. List the requested talent, strength and creative requirements you'll need to display. Reread Chapter Six for conditioning exercises. It is important you get your body to its peak physical condition.

Second, create skits appropriate for your traditional school mascot. Apply yourself using the sample training program below.

SAMPLE TRAINING PROGRAM FOR MASCOT TRYOUTS

Creative Drill—The creative drill is designed to advance and develop spontaneous, creative thinking processes in relation to the mascot character.

Time: 10 minutes

Starting position: Sit comfortably on a chair with both feet on the floor. Place your hands on your lap and close your eyes. Pretend you are a bear, tiger, hornet or eagle. Open your eyes and work through (imitating) the following:

How does the character move, prance, or run?
What kind of temperament does the character have?
How would the character act if it were young and playful?

1. Write what you've visualized down on a sheet of notebook paper.

2. List any aspects about the character that can be exaggerated.

Note: It is unwise and a bad habit to rely solely upon spontaneous creativity in place of practice, however you should write down spontaneous moves that worked well.

Spirit Drill—The spirit drill is designed to incorporate crowd participation into usable skit scenarios.

Time: 20 minutes

1. Take ten minutes to determine your ideal mascot theme presentation. Apply what you discovered from the creative drill to assist you in its preparation.

2. Spend the remaining ten minutes implementing your theme with the audience. Visualize an active audience. Work your audience into your theme to produce your desired effect. Be sure all your animated actions will generate positive crowd responses.

Finally, practice each day in front of a large mirror. Plan to use your own props and music if none are required. Ask your family or close friends to give you constructive criticism to help you improve. It will be hard, but try not to take criticism personally. Consider it a motivational challenge to do something greater. Don't hesitate or second guess yourself. You'll never know if you can do better unless you try. Successful training is a combination of good total health, traditional character development and practice. *Remember, you've got the potential and only you can unleash it.*

★ TRYOUTS

Every school selects its mascots differently. You will have to tryout and you may be judged by a sponsor, a spirit club committee or the cheerleading squad or coach. Tryouts are typically held at the same time as cheerleader tryouts. They usually last one day and result in the selection of a mascot and one alternate for the coming year.

Tryouts usually consist of a routine skit or dance performed to music. In some cases you will wear the costume during tryouts. Focus on your role at tryouts. Your role is to charm the audience. Don't worry if your hair is slightly out of place or if your friends' parents are watching. When your turn is called, take a deep breath and concentrate on using your time wisely.

You will be examined and judged as to how well your walk fits the traditional role of the mascot. Depending on how your tryout skit is constructed, you may take charge immediately or indirectly. Decide when and how you will use your arms and hands to emphasize your key points. Know ahead of time when to take the lead and have a good time. Let your enthusiasm show—it's contagious. Never underestimate your ability to win over an audience while in costume. Below is a sample of how you will be judged:

Sample Judging Sheet
Name _____ Number _____
Judge _____
Appearance _____ 5 points
Crowd Appeal _____ 15 points
Personality _____ 15 points
Motions _____ 10 points

Creativity _____ 15 points
Timing and Rhythm _____ 10 points
Style and Execution _____ 10 points
Overall Effectiveness _____ 20 points
TOTAL: _____ 100 points

★ CHARACTER ACTING

The character of the mascot is one of the trademarks of your school. The costume's vibrant facial expression has a lot to do with the personality you'll convey. Begin by outlining your desired message to the crowd. Some mascots are bold and mean, some are cool and funny and some are just plain crazy like the San Diego Chicken. Listed are five techniques for character development:

1. Incorporate exaggerated movements. Slow and deliberate movements are more eye-catching and expressive than quick, small ones. Many mascots create the joker-type personality by combining small, tiny steps in their routine. Quick, small movements can be incorporated when delivering the punch line to a funny skit you are acting out on the field. Hand gestures must be done so they can be seen on the sidelines. Consider adding hip movements to enhance the personality.

2. Create a walk of your own. Determine the walk of your mascot by the style of its feet and head. The school may have a traditional image for the mascot that may dictate how you walk. The larger your uniform's head and feet the slower the walk. Some feet will require you to pick your legs up higher than normal.

3. Encourage a sportsmanlike image. The audience expects you to be an entertainer and ambassador of good will. Remember, you are there to evoke team sprit and enthusiasm while having fun with the fans.

4. Concentrate on different game play scenarios. When the going gets tough, the crowd enjoys creativity. If your team has just scored, you may choose to imitate the scoring play for a repeat. Inspire positive action. Remember, the crowd is looking to you for fun.

5. Practice for peak performance. While in costume, spend time each week in front of a wall length mirror. Apply Chapter Six in your practice sessions with a careful heat acclimation program. It is very important to replenish your water loss during scheduled breaks or when necessary. It is dangerous to go without water for extended periods of time.

★ KEY DEVELOPMENT HINTS

1. Determine your mascot's character and have fun with it.

2. Animate your character with motions and gestures. Remember, they cannot see your face.

3. Encourage good sportsmanship.

4. Practice your walk and game scenarios.

5. Replenish water loss frequently.

★ MASCOT DYNAMICS IN A NUTSHELL

Mascot ingredients call for exuberant training with a dash of creative spontaneity. *Esprit de corps* is the primary responsibility of mascots at all required events. What's greatest about being a mascot? The audience will look to you for ecstatic motivational antics to get them out of the dumps. "I was shy," said Eppy the Eagle, "but in costume I was ruled by an uninhibited crazy side." As mascot, you can serve as a bridge between the crowd and cheerleaders. Mascots often assist the cheerleaders in alerting the audience for upcoming yells. They're special for their smashing ingenuity and inspirational ability to involve noncheering groups in vivacious revelry. Being a successful mascot means having explosive energy to keep the crowd roaring. As mascot you'll feel an immediate sense of personal and educational pride. Says Eppy, "Being the school mascot boosted my confidence and changed my life for the better."

CHAPTER 18

COLLEGIATE POM SQUADS

Cheerleading becomes more advanced at the collegiate level. College stunters perform fancy advanced and sharp elite stunts requiring members to have much more strength and power; the kind of power that has prompted men to return to the sidelines. Coed cheerleading squads are dominating colleges, and the fierce competition has turned many girls' attention towards pompon squads. That's good news for young women who like to dance and have an eye for professional cheerleading.

The shared support responsibilities of cheerleaders and pompon squads make them both valuable assets to every school. Pompon and dance teams are commonly referred to as "songleaders" because they originally helped to lead the school song. The primary goal of songleading, irrespective of the name, is to entertain the fans through dancing.

Although their earliest roots are with the drill teams of the '40s and '50s, one could argue that "songleaders" get their inspiration from the professional cheerleading squads of today. Pompon

squads are where traditional cheerleading meets professional style cheerleading. Some of their main responsibilities include dancing during official breaks of the game and special events, and they may even assist the cheerleaders in performing cheers along the sidelines.

★ ELIGIBILITY

In order to participate and assure your graduation, you must abide by the rules that have been established for all candidates. Eligibility status is obtained through the following general requirements:

Candidates must be accepted or enrolled in good standing at the college or university for the following year.

Tryouts are open to students attending full time with at least 12 credit-hours.

Candidates must have a cumulative grade point average of 2.0 or greater on a 4.0 scale. Normally, the more selective a squad is, the higher the GPA requirements will be.

★ MEMBERSHIP

Membership responsibilities include attending all home games, scheduled away games, special appearances, pep rallies and community events. No more than twelve members are allowed on the field or court for time-out performances.[1] To perform, members must be in peak physical condition. This element is crucial because the last routine must always look as energetic and fresh as the first.

★ CONDITIONING

Conditioning your heart and lungs for vigorous dancing will require you to take some of the exercises listed in Chapter Five to a scientific discipline. Start working on flattening your splits and high kicks and take some dance classes at least six months before tryouts if you need extra help. Practice these things early before it's too late.

★ CHOREOGRAPHY

Creative choreography is the life of the pompon squad. The routines must entertain the audience and be appropriate to each event. Squads perform to band or prerecorded music and select different styles to complement chosen themes. Each routine benefits when the choreography is flashy, has variety, pep, and displays good use of movement. Small, intricate dance steps are rarely appreciated on the football field because the audience is too far away to see them clearly. Small, intricate steps are more appropriate for the court and stage and most appreciated when repeated using the variation method. The use of visual aids such as novelty props, formations and contagions or "ripples" are highly effective for pom squads. For group choreography, the style and costume for the routine should always fit the preselected music and theme. Routines containing varied formations, props and costumes will add immediate life to your dance numbers.

★ TRYOUTS

Inquire early. Typically, tryouts are held in March or April with some in early September to allow eligible freshman to participate. Call or write for tryout information and an application to be mailed to your home address; or pick the materials up in person. Be sure to read the deadline for return.

Tryouts typically consist of one dance or pompon routine, a fight song number, and one original routine you will choreograph to your own music. In most cases, candidates will tryout in groups and then be asked to perform individual skills such as kicks and splits. Tryouts begin with a short general meeting followed by the tryout training clinic.

Clinics last between three days to one week. The clinic week will be instructional learning, with the final day open for review. Candidates will learn dance routines and the necessary basics expected for the audition. Routines are more advanced because they account for many different skills. You will be required to know splits, high kicks, leaps, turns and some jumps. Gymnastics are not necessary, but they are always helpful. Typical routines are jazz, funk or precision pompon. The choreographer will watch how quickly you learn, clean and polish your mistakes. You may feel somewhat burdened with so much learning material; your memory skills will certainly be challenged! Do your best to learn what you can on the spot, then go home and review your dance notes.

Your original tryout routine should represent your individual abilities as a dancer and performer. Here are a few key tips to think over before you choreograph your tryout routine.

Select music that is mixed. You can make a tape by mixing two or more songs on a dual cassette recorder.

Coordinate the music, theme, style and costume with your personality.

Keep your routine style similar to the style of the present squad.

Incorporate the latest sophisticated moves into your tryout routine.

Include tumbling or exceptional leaps into your routine at climactic moments in the music.

Make good use of the floor space available, and develop a dramatic ending.

Work on smooth transitions and variety.

Candidates will be judged on group routines, personal skills and showmanship. Be sure to dress appropriately for auditions. You'll want to look and dress your best. Wear a smile on your face and recover successfully if you make a mistake.

Practices are typically held three days a week for a minimum of three hours at a time. Successful squads engage their audience with smiles and facial expressions. Your ability to convey emotions through facial expression and body movements will set your squad apart from the rest.

★ PERFORMANCES

Squads should always have a good repertoire of routines. Songleader captains must communicate with head cheerleaders during events to assure orderly performances. Post a miniature game day schedule on your pompons and at the sidelines one hour before a game. Prepare both short and long numbers for each game according to the game agenda worked out with the cheerleaders and band director. Determine your places on the sidelines with full-out rehearsals to include the entrance, exit and sequence procedures for each routine.

The typical game plan contains between seven to ten routines for a football game, and six to eight routines for a court game. Pre-game shows are a great way to draw in the audience to be seated for the upcoming game and excellent times to showcase your best routines. Pre-games consist of one to two dance numbers. Time-out routines are performed throughout the game. Because routines may be cut short when play resumes on the field or court, time-out performances provide excellent opportunities to perform the fight song or a short routine. Combination routines with the band or flag corps make excellent half-time performances. Half-times consist of two to three longer performance numbers. To celebrate the thrill of victory or lift the spirits of fans in a disappointing defeat, post-game performances usually encompass the fight song, school song or an upbeat song immediately following the game. Typically, post-game performances are between one to two minutes. It's always a good idea to have a different routine ready for each possible outcome.

1 The National Collegiate Athletic Association. 1-AA Football Division Championship Handbooks (Overland Park, Kansas: NCAA, 1993).

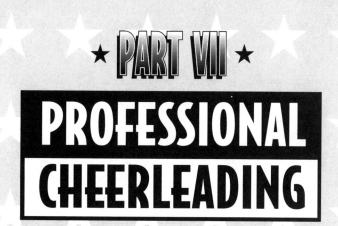

★ PART VII ★

PROFESSIONAL CHEERLEADING

★CHAPTER 19★

PROFESSIONAL CHEERLEADING

Professional football cheerleaders and basketball dance team members enjoy high profile positions in the world of professional sports. Participation on a professional squad leads to immediate local celebrity status, public recognition, T.V. and radio exposure and the ultimate fame and glamour that comes with the territory. Two world-famous professional squads have capitalized on this status, becoming stars in their own right. *The Dallas Cowboys Cheerleaders* made-for-television movie, filmed in 1978, and the *Los Angeles Lakers Girls* movie helped make these squads household names throughout the world.

Concurrently, professional cheerleading is a phenomenon that is sweeping across Japan. Japanese magazine columnist Yoshiyuki Sasaki writes, "Cheerleaders have come into the spotlight as American Football has increased in popularity. Groups learn dancing from professionals and copy cheerleading techniques from the Americans."[1] This heightened awareness and credibility have galvanized the attention of cor-

porate America as well as marketing and advertising firms from Los Angeles to Madison Avenue.

America's love affair with professional sports has become a multibillion dollar industry. Promotional goods have skyrocketed for the Dallas Cowboys Cheerleaders and requests for audition material have tripled. There are surging requests for audition information and promotional products for most all professional cheerleading groups. Many hopefuls travel thousands of miles across the country, and a few travel the world for a chance to audition for a professional squad.

Because there are so few professional cheerleaders, the knowledge and experience to cheer professionally is usually taken for granted and only passed on by word of mouth to friends. Most professional cheerleaders move on to other careers and become preoccupied with their daily lives. Many reach for similar careers once leaving cheerleading. Says Dawn Mycock, Director of the Philadelphia 76ers Dance Team, "Many of our members have moved on to similar careers in modeling and performing professionally." As the status profile and commercial relevance of professional cheerleading and dance squads has dramatically increased within the past few years, the successful candidate will need more than just hard work, talent or even pure luck. This chapter explains the crucial elements, strategies and insights you can employ to enhance the chances of being selected for that coveted position.

★ WHAT IS IT LIKE TO CHEER ON A PROFESSIONAL SQUAD?

People always ask me "what's it really like?" The truth is, only someone who puts on a uniform knows exactly how good it feels. There's a great rush of pride and self-accomplishment anytime you slip on a uniform for the first time. As a new professional squad member you're still just the same person as always inside—except now you're in a high profile position and fans will look up to you. When you're in a new limelight, people will hold you in high regard.

For example, many years ago and before I cheered for a professional team, I met a blonde, blue-eyed country girl, with an appearance that depicted the "All-American Girl." I put her, a Dallas Cowboys Cheerleader, on a pedestal as do sports fans who admire a particular athlete. Star struck, I actually carried her autographed photo in my purse everywhere I went because she was the closest I'd ever come to meeting someone famous.

★ HOW DOES PROFESSIONAL CHEERLEADING DIFFER FROM TRADITIONAL CHEERLEADING?

Professional cheerleading involves dance line entertainment for sports fans. Unlike traditional cheerleading where cheers and stunts are the norm, professional football cheerleaders specifically perform dance routines to lift the crowd's spirits with few chants involved. There are fans of all ages at the games as opposed to a general younger age group. The unknown faces in the crowd change from week to week at professional games, unlike traditional cheerleading where your peers are in the crowd. You also get a bit more television time as a professional cheerleader. As a professional squad member, there is greater community recognition, greater travel, and promotional work such as modeling.

Professional squads differ between football and basketball teams. Generally speaking, basketball squads perform tighter, more intricate dance moves and prefer to be recognized as "dancers." Football squads, having to compensate for distance, perform big motion, high energy, pompon routines. Because they are trained to perform on both field and stage, football cheerleading squads perform a greater range of themes, presentations, and styles for their shows. Basketball dance squads keep their performance routines structured for the hard floor surfaces. All teams, however, perform to "top forty" music. Some squads incorporate show tunes, oldies, cultural and novelty numbers.

Image

Just what type of image do successful professional squads portray to successfully capture attention and mystify the public? Public image is the life of the professional squad and has been the premature death of many squads over the past years. Organizations with the clearest, most established rules of behavior and who make public appearances at reputable locations tend to hold the highest public ratings over the long term; thus, they command more media attention. A squad is only as good as its image. The constant dilemma with a professional squad's image is that it takes a minimum four years to build and only one day to destroy it.

Expect rules regarding squad reputation and

image to be held in high regard by directors. Most squads have established strict rules and guidelines for members to follow both on duty and off. For many candidates, this dictates obeying rules that will seem very militaristic for those unaccustomed to rigorous discipline. These rules are meant to preserve and build the image of the squad.

One of the things I appreciated most while cheerleading with the Dallas Cowboys Cheerleaders was that we all acknowledged each other with a "yes, ma'am." Perfect etiquette in public appearances, manners, dress and makeup was the only way we did things. I really learned a lot. The grooming was an excellent improvement in my people skills.

★ IN CASE YOU WERE WONDERING . . .

What types of activities are involved outside of game day performances?

Performances may include national telethons and show appearances. Some organizations have special show squads made up of selected members. The show squads help handle the enormous requests for public appearances. Some travel extensively around the globe on entertainment tours, civic parades and public celebrations. Being selected for a show squad is a tremendous honor, and requires much more of your time. I personally enjoyed being a part of our show group because it gave me the opportunity to perform more often. However, some of the most rewarding experiences for me were the community service projects that we did as an entire squad. Typically, professional squads do a lot for their community by visiting hospitals and nursing homes and by charity fundraising.

Game travel is also requisite for football playoff games or the basketball all-star game. One squad member represents each squad at the Pro Bowl in Hawaii each year. Paid personal appearances to local business functions are scheduled by each squad director. Many squads publish or promote themselves through promotional calendars, posters, trading cards, billboards and television commercials.

How much are professional cheer and dance team member salaries?

Professional squad members must enjoy their position. Nancy Gerlach, director of the Buffalo Jills Cheerleaders, comments, "Our ladies do this strictly for their enjoyment. They do not get paid for cheering." But for the teams who do, the average remuneration is very minimal, ranging only between $15.00 and $65.00 per game. However, some teams do provide one or two game day tickets and paid appearance bonuses.

How important is character?

Very important. Team organizations want and need respectable young ladies who can handle the press, encourage the public, win the hearts of children and support the team at all costs. They must have members who will be committed to the squad, and whose personal commitments will not interfere. They are looking for young women with unique personalities that fit their image. Just remember, hiring directors are looking for individuals not clones.

What kind of muscle tone and fitness do hiring directors look for?

Directors are not looking for muscle-bound cheerleaders but very fit individuals. Performing for a professional team is exhausting. Keeping your position on the sidelines means being capable of withstanding fatigue.

Do veterans automatically make the squad each year?

No. If you are a border-line dancer, failed to follow the rules during the season, displayed a bad attitude or created a teammate problem, then you may not make it back. Directors want veterans who can teach and lead new rookies. Veterans are the "example setters" on the squad. Lisa Holtz-Odell, director of the Denver Nuggets Dancers explains, "Members must improve [during the year] and become technically clean dancers." It is simply a professional decision.

Is physical beauty important to judges?

Most will agree physical beauty is very helpful, but a truly beautiful person is one who is beautiful on the inside and has a warm charisma. She doesn't have to be the prettiest, but project good, strong dance ability, a well-rounded attitude and the desire to look her very best. Lisa Estrada, director of the Los Angeles Lakers Girls, comments on her feelings toward beauty, attitude and the importance for a strong performance. "That's not something I guide my auditions on; like is she really cute? I'd rather see a tight, talented squad out there more than I would seventeen beautiful girls who have two left feet. I would much rather have girls who can 'work it' and have a good time."

Are applications kept on file?

Generally not. With the enormous numbers auditioning from year to year, it requires too much effort and space for hiring directors to keep all requested applications on file. It would also be unusual for a squad director to call candidates back from applications after the new squad had been selected, even when the squad number drops after the starting season. I suggest you make a copy of your application and update it for the next year.

What guidelines can you expect?

Appropriate personal conduct is the most important goal. Directors expect complete commitment to rehearsals, games and appearances. Any act of insubordination will result in a disciplinary action. Tardiness to rehearsals may cause you to be benched, and if you miss a game or a rehearsal without a pardonable excuse, you may be dismissed from the squad. Each member is responsible for proper grooming and is not allowed to make any drastic changes in appearance. Members must replace uniform items if damaged, lost or stolen. There is no gum chewing, smoking, drinking, jewelry or hair curlers allowed while in public uniform. Most all squads dictate no fraternizing with players or coaches as a squad member. People will ask you to make guest appearances, but all appearances must be scheduled through the administration office. Being a professional squad member is an elite privilege and with it come some trade-offs, but anyone who is a pro cheerleader will tell you it's one of the best times of their life.

Do squad members receive fan mail?

Most do, and many teams encourage or require members to send a small reply to those who take the time to write. The fans are made up of children, parents, service men and women, grandparents and curious people from all over the world. Many request photos or they are kind enough to send photos that they took at a recent game. Although cheerleaders do not expect or ask to receive gifts, some fans will send flowers and homemade items. Most fans just want to tell you of a job well done and how you are their favorite. For the most part, receiving fan mail will become some of your most cherished memories as a cheerleader.

★ AUDITIONS

Becoming a professional squad member will require more head-to-head competition than probably anything you have ever done. You can not be intimidated in showing off your very best star qualities. Mary Barnes, Los Angeles Raiderettes Coordinator, acknowledges, "The ladies with real star qualities are noticed and have the advantage but the shy girls that make the squad develop those star qualities over time. They learn their hair, their makeup, and to do with what they have. They begin as sweet little girls who would not have stopped the show but now, as they get older, they definitely would have."

Audition Requirements

Requirements will vary between organizations and each squad will give you their specific expectations that will fall somewhere within the requirements listed below.

Possess at least one to five years of dance experience

You must be at least 18 years of age (or older for some squads)

Must have proportionate height and weight

Must be willing to relocate to the area

Must be able to attend all required gatherings, including one to six rehearsals per week

How to Apply

When are tryouts? Generally auditions for professional football squads are held in the months of March through May. Basketball dancer auditions follow a different schedule appropriate to their season. Their auditions are typically held late July through early September. Contact the squad(s) you are interested in for application information as soon as their playing season ends. Send a SASE for an application and tryout material and don't delay. Many organizations have requirements that must be met prior to the audition application date. Many teams have audition hotlines set up one month before auditions to give locations and other pertinent information.

Photos

Organizations are usually specific when it comes to pictures. Always submit the photo that is sug-

gested. A head shot should include head and shoulders only. Try to eliminate any background distractions that could take away from you. These photos do *not* have to be professional portraits, but because you want to be a professional, you will want to select a picture that will sell you at your very best. Always wear an even amount of makeup and lipstick. Brush your hair smooth, and pull it away from your eyes. Sincerity always shows best in your eyes, so let them sparkle. Curls and hair spray are fine, but don't overdo. Hair should never take up more picture space than your head itself. If you wear jewelry, limit it to small earrings only. Best to wear studs. A full body shot in leotards or otherwise specified outfit can be taken in numerous ways. There are no hard and fast rules here. I suggest a standing ¾-side front pose. It will accent your figure and hide the unwanted bulges you are still working on.

PICKY PICTURE POINTERS

Always submit the photo they request.

Wear exactly what is requested.

Smile, keep your head up, shoulders and neck relaxed and hold your stomach in.

Resumes

The resume is gaining in popularity. Resumes have been widely used in areas of California and New York where dance professionals are hired for their expertise in television, films and theater.

Your resume must highlight your achievements even if you have only moderate experience. Highlight your strongest qualifications first. Do not miss any opportunities to persuade. Remember, how you present your experience may be more important than the experience itself. Give specific information and make sure it is true. It is common for high profile organizations to conduct background checks and review references. Memorize your resume; it is what they know about you!

RESUME ELEMENTS:

Personal Information—Provide your name, address and phone numbers during the day and evening.

Education—List your educational background degrees held, and special courses worthy of mention. Provide the name of schools and dates attended. If you expect a degree, provide the anticipated graduation date and the degree.

Experience—Describe your experience in the field, employment information and a one-line description of the type of positions you have held. List the skills and leadership positions you have obtained.

Personal Achievements—List your hobbies, awards and volunteer work.

References—Offer references, providing the names, addresses and telephone numbers of reputable sources who can vouch for you.

Your resume should highlight the most recent or most impressive activities for the position first. There is no single correct way of presenting a resume, but there are ways a resume can help you get noticed. Your resume should appear as clean and neat as possible. Type your resume on a word processor or very good typewriter. Use sharp print and avoid corrections on the final draft. Allow for adequate spacing, and select one-inch margins on equal sides. It is always best to attach a photo at the top.

Sample Resume

Jane Doe
156 Byrne Street
Lone Star, Texas 75668
(903) 555-1265

Experience: Drill Team Director, Eisenhower High School 1994-present, Dallas Cowboys Cheerleaders 1990–1993, Manchester Drill Team

Captain 1989, Gymnastics; District Champions 1989.

Education: Bachelor of Arts Degree; dance and performance Maritime University 1993

Special Training: Calson art clinic for ballet and jazz; an intensive one month training in Jazz dance movements, Mason's methods of self-motivation and leadership course; an insightful study into motivating and leading those around you. Proficiency in French; taught myself with a home study course.

Personal Achievements: Christianson dance television video productions; premier dancer 1994, Jackie Andrews Award for leadership 1993, Best Dancer of the Year Award 1993, Maritime pom squad captain 1993, Miss Manchester High School 1988.

References available upon request

Pre-Audition Workshops

Many teams offer dance workshops several months prior to auditions to help prepare candidates. These help you get used to the choreographer's style and teaching methods, but your attendance also allows them to prejudge you before auditions. Prejudgment can be good if you're an excellent dancer who polishes quickly or bad if you don't dance well or if your attendance during the class is erratic. Decide for yourself. I believe it is a good idea to attend at least one session. I encourage you to also take comparable dance lessons regularly for several months until your audition day.

Typical Auditions Order

The typical audition order of professional squads varies in length from one full day to three full days. Some squads take more time to make the last few cuts than others. If traveling, plan for accommodations if the organization is requiring candidates to return for further extensive auditions or camp. The following is a brief description of what to expect:

1. Preliminaries—Typically, you will learn a short combination or be asked to perform freestyle (ad-lib) to music.

2. Semifinals—You may be taught a combination and will be asked to display technical skills such as high kicks and splits.

3. Finals—You may be asked to perform an original routine at this stage of tryouts. Finals may include an extensive interview, personal essay and a sports and current events quiz.

Choreographer's Checklist

At finals, many directors will expect you to choreograph a routine of your own. Please review Chapter Fourteen for choreography elements. The following is a choreographer's checklist to follow when choreographing your original routine for tryouts:

1. Have you coordinated your music, style, theme and costume?

2. Have you included necessary dance elements? Try to incorporate leaps, high kicks, turns, jumps and tumbling (if you are capable).

3. Have you cleaned and perfected each step? Movements are flashy and exciting? Transitions are smooth? Movements are easy to see from a distance?

4. Have you prepared an adequate surprise ending?

5. Have you made sure there is adequate space for the routine in the audition room?

6. Have you rehearsed the performance material?

7. Have you prepared the routine to the specified guidelines? Style is proper per request? Music fits exactly within the specific amount of time given?

If you get discouraged, just continue to work at improving yourself. Lisa Holtz-Odell, director of the Denver Nuggets Dancers, admits, "I will take a less capable dancer with a better attitude because I can make anyone a good dancer."

The Audition Day

Wear exactly what is required. It is not uncommon for girls who traveled a great distance to be turned away at auditions because they did not follow instructions or find out the proper attire guidelines for tryouts. Arrive one to two hours early because lines are long. Allow adequate time to drive through traffic, park, wait in line for registration and begin warming your body up. Upon arriving, find the proper line and sign in at registration. Your competition and tryout order numbers will be issued and you will be assigned to a group. Be sure to review all required dance material.

Judging

Your behavior at this point is important and you will be noticed whether you know it or not. Concentrate on smiling, being polite and helpful to the other candidates. Don't engage in gossip; instead, show you are a good sport and wish others well. Monique Alhaddad sums up the judging by most squads very concisely and completely. As director of the Indiana Pacemates, the first professional Dance/Cheer squad in the NBA and the first squad ever to perform at an NBA All Star Game, Monique points out, "Members must have good attitudes, be enthusiastic, possess dance ability, and have the ability to pick up quick." The following score sheet will give you a good idea of how directors judge those who have come to audition. It differs slightly from the others:

Sample Judges Score Sheet
Candidate# _____ Judge# _____
Attitude
Confidence (1–5) _____
Interaction With Others (1–5) _____
Showmanship
Eye Contact (1–10) _____
Facial Expressions (1–10) _____
Dance Ability
Technique (1–10) _____
Energy Level (1–10) _____
Learning Ability (1–10) _____
Displayed Skills (1–10) _____
Appearance
Poise (1–10) _____
Face (1–10) _____
Figure (1–10) _____
Total Possible Points 100
TOTAL SCORE _____

AUDITION PREPARATION EXERCISES:
To help prepare you for the audition process, practice the following exercises.

Prepare a two minute polished theme routine to music under a two week deadline for completion.

Practice freestyle dancing to various types of music.

Read the latest team yearbook and write out a summary of key points regarding the franchise team and squad.

Read the newspaper and sports section daily. Stay current on events and happenings.

Video record yourself in a mock interview and review it for improvement. Watch out for posture, speaking ability, positive attitude and your smile.

★ DARE TO DREAM

Professional squads provide opportunities for a member to be a role model for many young people with your same dreams and hopes of becoming a cheerleader. The only limits you have in front of you are the ones you put before yourself, because for every dreamer there is a star waiting to be wished upon. In your quest to become a professional cheerleader, keep in mind the viewpoint of Leslie Matz, director of the Philadelphia Eagles Cheerleaders, "We have two cheerleaders on our squad with hearing impairments and they are excellent performers. If someone has a dream to try out, she should not let anyone or anything stop her from doing so!"

Remember, it takes a dreamer to make a dream come true!

★ PROFESSIONAL CHEERLEADING AND DANCE TEAM DIRECTORY

NFL CHEERLEADING SQUADS

Atlanta Falcons
Atlanta Falcons Cheerleaders
Suwanee Road &I85
Suwanee, GA 30174
Contact: Ginger Poole
(404) 945–1111

Buffalo Bills
Buffalo Jills Cheerleaders
One Bills Drive
Orchard Park, NY 14127
Contact: Nancy Gerlach
(716) 648–1800

Cincinnati Bengals
Cincinnati Ben Gals
200 Riverfront Stadium
Cincinnati, OH 45202
(513) 621–3550

Dallas Cowboys
Dallas Cowboys Cheerleaders
One Cowboys Parkway
Irving, TX. 75063
Contact: Kelli McGonagill
(214) 556–9900

Denver Broncos
Denver Broncos Cheerleaders
13655 Broncos Park
Englewood, CO 80112
Contact: Jay Howarth
(303) 649–9000
(Write in for information only)

Houston Oilers
Houston Oilers Derrick Dolls
6910 Fannin Street
Houston, Texas 77030
Contact: Cindy Villarreal-
    Hughes
(713) 797–9111

Indianapolis Colts
Indianapolis Colts Cheerleaders
7001 West 56th Street
Indianapolis, IN 46254
Contact: Pamela Humphrey
(317) 297–2658

Kansas City Chiefs
Kansas City Chiefs Cheerleaders
One Arrowhead Drive
Kansas City, MO 64129
Contact: Donna Scott
(816) 924–9300

Los Angeles Raiders
Los Angeles Raiderettes
332 Center Street
El Segundo, CA 90245
Contact: Mary Barnes
(310) 322–3451

Squad video available (800)
    226–4775

Los Angeles Rams
*Los Angeles Rams Cheerleaders
    and Stunt Team*
2327 Lincoln Avenue
Anaheim, CA 92801
Contact: Keely Fimbres
(714) 535–7267

Miami Dolphins
Miami Dolphin Cheerleaders
2269 NW. 199th Street
Miami, FL 33056
Contact: Kathy Shashaty
(305) 620–5000

Minnesota Vikings
Minnesota Viking Cheerleaders
9520 Viking Drive
Eden Prairie, MN 55344
Contact: Mary Ann Dallas
(612) 828–6500

New England Patriots
Patriettes
Route One Foxboro Stadium
Foxborough, MA 02035
Contact: Lisa Coles
(508) 543–8200

New Orleans Saints
Saintsations
1500 Poydras Street
New Orleans, LA. 70112
Contact: Silvia Alfortish
(504) 733–0255

Philadelphia Eagles
Philadelphia Eagles Cheerleaders
Veterans Stadium
3501 S. Broad Street

Philadelphia, PA 19148
Contact: Leslie Matz
(215) 463–2500

Phoenix Cardinals
Cardinals Heat Wave
P.O. Box 888
Phoenix AZ. 85001
Contact: Vickie Pheiffer
(602) 379–0101

San Diego Chargers
2133 Leghorn Street
Mountain View, CA 94043
Contact: USA Productions
(415) 969–6660

San Francisco 49ers
2133 Leghorn Street
Mountain View, CA 94043
Contact: USA Productions
(415) 969–6660

Seattle Seahawks
Sea Gals
11220 NE. 53rd Street
Kirkland, WA 98033
Contact: Sandy Gregory
(206) 827–9777

Tampa Bay Buccaneers
Swashbuclers
One Buccaneer Place
Tampa, FL 33607
Contact: Sherry Gruden
(813) 870–2700

NBA DANCE TEAMS

Atlanta Hawks
Atlanta Hawks Dance Team
One CNN Center NW
3 Tower, Suite 405

Atlanta, GA 30335
Contact: Donna Feazell
(404) 827–3800

Charlotte Hornets
The Honey Bees
One Hive Drive
Charlotte, NC 28217
Contact: Tracy Wheeler
(704) 357–0252

Chicago Bulls
Luvabulls
908 N. Michigan Ave.
Suite 1600
Chicago, IL 60611
Contact: Kathy Core
(312) 943–5800

Cleveland Cavaliers
Cavs Dance Team
The Coliseum
2923 Streetsboro Road
Richfield, OH 44286
Contact: Mark Heffernan
(216) 659–9100

Dallas Mavericks
Dallas Mavericks Dancers
Reunion Arena
777 Sports Street
Dallas, Texas 75207
Contact: Joyce Pennington
(214) 748–1808

Denver Nuggets
Denver Nuggets Dancers
P.O. Box 4658
Denver, CO 89204
Contact: Lisa Holtz-Odell
(303) 893–6700

Golden State Warriors
Warrior Girls
2133 Leghorn Street
Mountain View, CA 94043
Contact: USA Productions
(415) 969–6660

Houston Rockets
Houston Rockets Dance Team
10 Greenway Plaza
Houston, Texas 77046
Contact: Tracy Mitchell
(713) 627–0600

Indiana Pacers
Indiana Pacemates
300 East Market Street
Indianapolis, IN 46224
Contact: Monique Alhaddad
(317) 263–2100

Los Angeles Clippers
Los Angeles Clippers
2133 Leghorn Street
Mountain View, CA 94043
Contact: USA Productions
(415) 969–6660

Los Angeles Lakers
Los Angeles Laker Girls
The Great Western Forum
3900 W. Manchester Blvd.
Inglewood, CA 90305
Contact: Lisa Estrada
(310) 419–3100

Miami Heat
Miami Heat Dancers
Miami Arena
721 NW. First Ave.
Miami, FL. 33136
Contact: Sanin Hightower
(305) 577–4328

Milwaukee Bucks
Energy
1001 N. Fourth Street
Milwaukee, WI 53203
Contact: Lois Wagner
(414)227–0500

Minnesota Timberwolves
*Minnesota Timberwolves
  Performance Team*
730 Hennepin Avenue, Suite
  500
Minneapolis, MN 55403
Contact: Sandy Sweetser
(612) 673–1600

New Jersey Nets
Jersey Girls
Meadowlands Arena
E. Rutherford, NJ 07073
Contact: Jenny Kerner
(201) 935–8888

New York Knickerbockers
New York City Dancers
Madison Square Garden
Two Pennsylvania Plaza
New York, NY 10001
Contact: Petra Belton
(212) 465–5867

Orlando Magic
Magic Girls
One Magic Place
Orlando, FL 32801
Contact: Darla Hancock
(407) 649–3200

Philadelphia 76ers
76ers Dance Team
P. O. Box 25040
Philadelphia, PA 19147

Contact: Dawn Mycock
(215) 339 –7600

Phoenix Suns
2910 N. Central
Phoenix, AZ 85012
Contact: Marless Stahle
(602) 379–7900

Portland Trail Blazers
Blazer Dance Team
700 NE. Multnomah, Suite 600
Portland, OR 97232
Contact: José Ayala
(503) 234–9291

Sacramento Kings
2133 Leghorn Street

Mountain View, CA 94043
Contact: USA Productions
(415) 969–6660

San Antonio Spurs
Silver Dancers
600 E. Market Street, Suite 102
San Antonio, TX 78205
Contact: Lori McDowell
(210) 554–7787

Seattle Supersonics
Seattle Supersonics Dance Team
190 Queen Anne Avenue
Seattle, WA 98109
Contact: Rob Martin
(206) 281–5850

Utah Jazz
Utah Jazz Dance Team
5 Triad Center
Suite 500
Salt Lake City, UT 84101
Contact: Katherine McCann
(801) 575–7800

Washington Bullets
Bullettes
Capitol Center
One Harry S. Truman Drive
Washington, DC 20875
Contact: Carla Kemp
(301) 622–3865

[1] Yoshiyuki Sasaki, "Swing those pompoms." *Pacific Friend* 20:9 (1992): 46–47.

★ PART VIII ★

LIFE AFTER CHEERLEADING

"I want to be a cheerleader forever." I hear this sentiment expressed in a thousand different ways. Fortunately, the qualities we've learned as cheerleaders have given us so many skills that make us extremely valuable in other careers. Leaving something we love is never easy, but if we take something good from it, life becomes so much more fulfilling. If there is one last thing to remember after reading my book, it is that cheerleading isn't something that ends, it stays deep inside our hearts and souls cheering us on through life!

★CHAPTER 20★

HOW TO TAKE ADVANTAGE OF YOUR EXPERIENCE

By providing you with instant success among peers, cheerleading raises your confidence and gives you a special distinction that you did not have before. Most cheerleaders are determined individuals who strive to achieve above the average in every aspect of their lives. But did you know our business and community leaders also play a cheerleading role? Corporate executives are cheerleaders for their corporations, rallying everyone to work together more efficiently to lower costs. The President of the United States acts as a cheerleader to bolster confidence in plans he wants passed through Congress. An Army general is a cheerleader who raises morale and directs troops. The entrepreneur is a cheerleader who takes on the odds to steer his small business in order to win the customers' loyalty. Overcoming the competition through teamwork and positive determination is valid in cheerleading and business. You see, all the same inner qualities that make you a good cheerleader become even more important as you move on to more permanent things. Your life is yours to make the very best of it you can.

★MAKING USE OF YOUR CHEERLEADING EXPERIENCE

There are many ways you can benefit from your cheerleading experience to receive financial compensation.

Camp Personnel

Many associations hire athletic trainers, office assistants, judges and instructors. Instructors teach camps and clinics from the elementary through collegiate level. Working for an association during the training months will entail professional commitment, some travel and long but rewarding hours of hard work with younger cheerleaders. You must enjoy working with others, be proficient in your cheerleading skills and have a deep desire to teach. Spirit associations hire individuals they can send to teach the latest moves and trends to cheerleaders abroad. Cheerleading has made its way to Europe, Mexico, Canada and Japan, and learning a language can open this and many doors for you now and in the future. Teaching a camp is a great way to see the world and do what you love best. For more information, contact the cheerleading associations listed in Appendix C.

Private Instructor

Consider teaching cheerleading at local cheer and dance studios or work independently with schools in your community. As a private instructor, you can assist squads or individual squad members develop cheerleading skills.

College Scholarships

Why not a scholarship in cheerleading? Since the passage of Title IX, many colleges now offer scholarships to cheerleaders. If you are looking at colleges, plan to continue with spiritleading and are seeking financial assistance, a college scholarship is one great way to help you narrow down your choices. The amounts vary between schools; they are typically small awards, but all scholarships provide some financial support and prestige as well.

But be careful not to major in cheerleading and minor in school. Your main focus in going to college is to get good grades while earning your degree; cheerleading comes second. Without good grades there will be no cheerleading for you in school. It's important to plan for your future. Make the most out of your education.

Be methodical as you narrow down the schools of your choice by using the following criteria. Begin by concentrating on your entrance credentials by maximizing your grades, SAT and ACT scores. Take the entrance exams at least one year before graduation to allow yourself adequate time to improve your scores if they do not meet the school's standards. Determine if geographic location is important for you and your family. Locate colleges with strong departments in the fields of your interest. Call them for general admission, student information packages. Review your credentials and admission requirements with a school counselor. As a general rule of thumb, private institutions and out-of-state schools will have higher tuition costs than a public institution in your home state. That is not to discourage you, but to encourage you to seek additional scholarships, grants and financial aid to help you afford costly tuition costs. Many coaches will help cheerleaders apply for financial assistance. Base your decision upon quality of education, proximity to family, financial aid, activities available and long-range goals.

Please see Appendix A. It provides a listing of universities who offer scholarships for cheerleading, mascot and pom squad positions.

WHEN SEEKING ASSISTANCE:

Call the college athletic department or student activities office.

Ask how many scholarships are awarded to cheerleaders, mascots or dance squad members.

Ask if they also assist in applying for financial aid for you if you are selected.

Ask for an application and information package.

COLLEGE SELECTION:

Make a checklist and select three colleges.

Visit prospective campuses.

Speak to other students.

Visit a practice or game.

Inquire about financial aid, review housing and student services.

Review your college catalog.

★ YOUR CAREER

What careers are suited for former cheerleaders who want to stay associated with cheerleading? Perhaps coaching, teaching full-time as an educator or taking advantage of your quality speaking skills. Try to develop your professional skills with the same zeal that you have developed your cheerleading skills. Then ask yourself, "How much do I want to stay within the field of cheerleading? What is it about cheerleading that I love?" Only you can answer that. As with many things, there is a time to reflect upon our achievement and continue to move forward instead of reliving the past. We must use our experience to influence others in our community, the workplace and family.

Look for the same aspects you love in cheerleading when deciding on a career. Consider the marketable skills you've obtained as a cheerleader: public speaking, directing, organizing, researching, public relations, social service and selling. The opportunities are better today than they ever have been for people who radiate positive attitudes and have a winner's outlook on the future. Opportunities are much better for you when you display the right attitude. For example, sales people must compete to win orders over their competition. They experience the same feelings of victory and are paid bonuses for their victories. Attorneys command attention in the courtroom when battling a case. Don't be afraid to pour your heart into something new. Remember your first victory in cheerleading was the first step toward your successful life. Common cheerleader qualities such as determination and the tenacity to succeed against all odds are extremely desirable in today's business and professional world.

Just what are employers looking for, and what will you need to succeed? One recruiter from a large corporation said, "Cheerleaders have what it takes for a challenging position in industry. They have displayed their ability to manage extremely hectic schedules; they have the high energy to succeed in the demanding job environment. They are usually capable of handling several responsibilities at one time which is crucial for business management. We like the balance that cheerleaders have developed in their lives."

Recruiters are looking for the same qualities as coaches looked for in selecting new squad members. They want responsible individuals of strong character, ethics and integrity, with the willingness to work hard as a team. They want achievers. And cheerleaders bring optimism and the pure will to win into the work place of their organizations. Those inner qualities cannot be taught on the job but must be learned through life's experiences.

Whether it be a job, career opportunity or a business start-up loan, the door opens when you convince the right people to believe in you. It's up to you to impress upon them your positive outlook and enthusiasm. This is wisdom you now can share with the key people to open the doors to your future.

So how do I choose what career is best for me, and which skills will be most desirable? The following Career-Skill Assessment will help you determine the relationship between your cheerleader skills and a future career.

★ CAREER-SKILL ASSESSMENT

Outlined are steps to help direct you to possible career paths. Grab a note pad and paper and begin by brainstorming.

1. List all your beneficial skills.

2. Analyze your skills in terms of professional experience.

3. Write down some interests in possible careers.

4. If they can benefit from your experience, list them in order of importance.

Now that you have the basic idea, start networking with people in the field.

★WHAT'S NEXT?

Cheerleading will soon be a fond memory and what will you do next? It is difficult to make decisions when the future holds so many possibilities. You are lucky to have the experiences as a cheerleader that have taught you how to make positive decisions regarding your future. You understand how to make people believe in you and have learned how to work when it was only you that cared enough to get the job done. You understand how to motivate people to come together for a common cause even when it seems hopeless. You also understand the importance of good morale and teamwork. You have become a better judge of character than most persons your age because of your sacrifice and hard work.

There are many non-cheerleading related jobs that would love a person with the skills demonstrated as a cheerleader. Public relations, advertising, marketing, sales and any form of public service would be highly suitable.

Wherever your ambitions and dreams take you, the experiences of having been a cheerleader will be some of the fondest and proudest moments of your life. Now the character you have developed because of those experiences must be fulfilled and allowed to flourish in a world full of opportunity. Keep a motivating spirit, for all those around you will depend on it! When deciding on which fork in the road to take, use your instinct and good logic; seek advice to make the solid decisions. Life is just beginning for you; it only gets better.

★ PART IX ★

APPENDICES

SCHOLARSHIP RESOURCES

The following are colleges and universities who also offer spirit scholarships to qualifying individuals.

★ALABAMA

JACKSONVILLE STATE UNIVERSITY
105 Bibbgraves
Jacksonville, Alabama 36265
Contact: Don Schmitts—Athletics
Phone: (205) 782–5006
Awards
Cheerleading: 50% tuition
Pompon: None
Mascot: 50% tuition
Squads: Varsity
Eligibility: 2.0 GPA   Freshmen eligible? No

SNEAD STATE JUNIOR COLLEGE
P.O. Drawer D
Boaz, Alabama 35757
Contact: Libby Bates—Athletics
Phone: (205) 593–5210

Awards
Cheerleading: Full tuition
Pompon: Full tuition
Mascot: None
Squads: Varsity
Eligibility: 2.0 GPA   Freshmen eligible? Yes

UNIVERSITY OF ALABAMA
P.O. Box 87032
Tuscaloosa, Alabama 35487–0373
Contact: Debbie Brown—Athletics
Phone: (205) 348–3636
Awards
Cheerleading: $500–$800
Pompon: $200 per year
Mascot: $250 JV; $1600 Varsity
Squads: JV, Varsity
Eligibility: 2.0 GPA   Freshmen eligible? Yes

★ARKANSAS

SOUTHERN ARKANSAS UNIVERSITY
S.A.U., P.O. Box 1330

Magnolia, Arkansas 71753
Contact: Roger Dunlap—Student Affairs
Phone: (501) 234–5120
Awards
Cheerleading: $300
Pompon: None
Mascot: None
Squads: Varsity
Eligibility: 2.0 GPA   Freshmen eligible? Yes

UNIVERSITY CENTRAL ARKANSAS
Office of Student Activities
U.C.A., Box 5101
Conway, Arkansas 72035
Contact: Jenny Taylor—Student Activities
Phone: (501) 450–3137
Awards
Cheerleading: 50% tuition
Pompon: None
Mascot: None
Squads: Varsity
Eligibility: 2.0 GPA   Freshmen eligible? No

UNIVERSITY OF ARKANSAS AT LITTLE ROCK
2801 South University
Little Rock, Arkansas 72204
Contact: Candice Zinn—Athletics
Phone: (501) 569–3167
Awards
Cheer/Dance Squad—One semester tuition
Mascot: None
Squads: Varsity
Eligibility: 2.0 GPA   Freshmen eligible? Yes

UNIVERSITY OF ARKANSAS AT PINE BLUFF
U.A.P.B., Box 126
Pine Bluff, Arkansas 71603
Contact: Karen Scott—Student Affairs
Phone: (501) 543–8405
Awards
Cheerleading: $1725; (only two scholarships
   available)
Pompon: None

Mascot: None
Squads: Varsity
Eligibility: 2.3 GPA   Freshmen eligible? Yes

★ CALIFORNIA

FRESNO STATE UNIVERSITY
4245 E. Hampton Way
Fresno, California 93726
Contact: Joyce Duncan—Athletics
Phone: (209) 278–2643
Awards
Cheerleading: $200
Pompon: $200
Mascot: $200
Squads: Varsity
Eligibility: 2.0 GPA   Freshman eligible? Yes

SAN FRANCISCO STATE UNIVERSITY
2130 Fulton Street
San Francisco, California 94117–1080
Contact: Margaret Baptista—Athletics
Phone: (415) 666–6891
Awards
Cheerleading: $850–1,000
Pompon: None
Mascot: None
Eligibility: 2.0 GPA   Freshmen Eligible? Yes

★ DELAWARE

DELAWARE STATE UNIVERSITY
1700 North Dupont Highway
Dover, Delaware, 19901
Contact: Anita Brinkley—Athletics
Phone: (302) 739–4928
Awards
Cheerleading: $500, books
Pompon: $500, books
Mascot: None
Squads: Varsity
Eligibility: 2.0 GPA, 1 year service
Freshmen eligible? Yes

★ DISTRICT OF COLUMBIA

GEORGE WASHINGTON UNIVERSITY
Smith Center
600 22nd Street, N.W.
Washington, D.C. 20052
Contact: John Kelly—Athletics
Phone: (202) 994–5972
<u>Awards</u>
Cheerleading: $1000–$3000
Pompon: None
Mascot: $1000–$3000
Squads: JV, Varsity
Eligibility: 2.0 GPA   Freshmen eligible? No

★ FLORIDA

UNIVERSITY OF FLORIDA AT GAINSVILLE
P.O. Box 14485
Gainsville, Florida 32604–2485
Contact: Jim Thorpe—Athletics
Phone: (904) 375–4683
<u>Awards</u>
Cheerleading: $180–$400
Pompon: None
Mascot: $375 per semester
Squads: JV, Varsity
Eligibility: 2.5 GPA   Freshmen eligible? Yes

JACKSONVILLE UNIVERSITY
2800 University Blvd. North
Jacksonville, Florida 32211
Contact: Angie Hollis—Student Activities
Phone: (904) 744–7374
<u>Awards</u>
Cheerleading: None
Pompon: Partial tuitition
Mascot: None
Squads: JV
Eligibility: 2.0 GPA   Freshmen eligible? Yes

UNIVERSITY OF MIAMI
Cheerleading Department
P.O. Box 248187
Coral Gables, Florida 33124–5240
Contact: Dan Reynolds—Athletics
Phone: (305) 284–5212
<u>Awards</u>
Cheerleading: $1000
Pompon: $1000
Mascot: $1000
Squads: JV, Varsity
Eligibility: 2.0 GPA, full-time status
Freshman eligible? No

★ HAWAII

HAWAII PACIFIC UNIVERSITY
1188 Fort Street, Suite 105
Honolulu, Hawaii 96813
Contact: Kim Clay—Athletics
Phone: (808) 544–1127
<u>Awards</u>
Cheerleading: 80–100% tuition
Pompon: None
Mascot: None
Squads: Varsity
Eligibility: 2.0 GPA   Freshmen eligible? Yes

★ ILLINOIS

COLLEGE OF SAINT FRANCIS
500 Wilcox
Jallette, Illinois 60435
Contact: Cindy Tyler—Athletics
Phone: (815) 729–3336
<u>Awards</u>
Cheerleading: $1000
Pompon: $1000
Mascot: $1000
Squads: Varsity
Eligibility: 2.0 GPA   Freshmen eligible? No

SOUTHERN ILLINOIS UNIVERSITY AT CARBONDALE
Intercollegiate Athletics
Lingle Hall, Room 118
Carbondale, Illinois 62901–6620
Contact: Nancy Eslung—Athletics
Phone: (618) 536–5566
<u>Awards</u>
Cheerleading: $125–400 per semester tuition
 credit
Pompon: $125–400 per semester tuition credit
Mascot: None
Squad: Varsity
Eligibility: 2.0 GPA   Freshmen eligible? No

UNIVERSITY OF ILLINOIS AT CHICAGO CIRCLE
400 South Peoria, Room 2250
Chicago, Illinois 60607
Contact: Rick Harrigan—Athletics
Phone: (312) 996–2772
<u>Awards</u>
Cheerleading: None
Pompon: None
Mascot: One semester tuition waiver
Squad: Varsity
Eligibility: 2.0 GPA   Freshmen eligible? Yes

★IOWA

TEIKYO WESTMAR UNIVERSITY
1002 Third Avenue S.E.
LeMars, Iowa 51031
Contact: Diane Terpstra—Athletics
Phone: (800) 352–4634, ext. 2614
<u>Awards</u>
Cheerleading: $1000 per semester
Pompon: $1000 per semester
Mascot: None
Squads: Varsity
Eligibility: 2.0 GPA   Freshmen eligible? Yes

★KANSAS

BUTLER COUNTY COMMUNITY COLLEGE
c/o Athletic Department, BCCC
901 South Haverhill
El Dorado, Kansas 67042
Contact: Robin Day—Athletics
Phone: (316) 321–2222
<u>Awards</u>
Cheerleading: $32 per credit hour
Pompon: $32 per credit hour
Mascot: $32 per credit hour
Squads: Varsity
Eligibility: 2.0 GPA   Freshman eligible? Yes

FORT HAYS STATE UNIVERSITY
600 Park Street
Hays, Kansas 67601
Contact: Terry Siek—Athletics
Phone: (800) 628–3478
<u>Awards</u>
Cheerleading: $740 Dorm credit
Pompon: None
Mascot: $740 Dorm credit
Squads: JV, Varsity
Eligibility: 2.0 GPA   Freshmen eligible? Yes

STERLING COLLEGE
Box 123
Sterling, Kansas 67579
Contact: Gail Prutow—Athletics
Phone: (316) 278–2905
<u>Awards</u>
Cheerleading: $250 per semester
Pompon: None
Mascot: None
Squads: Varsity
Eligibility: 2.2 GPA   Freshmen eligible? Yes

WICHITA STATE UNIVERSITY
1849 North Fairmont
Wichita, Kansas 67260–0126
Contact: Kelly Lewis—Athletics

Phone: (316) 689–3265

<u>Awards</u>

Cheerleading: $500 per semester

Pompon: None

Mascot: None

Squads: Varsity

Eligibility: 2.0 GPA   Freshmen eligible? Yes

★KENTUCKY

CUMBERLAND COLLEGE

Office of Administrations Cumberland College

Williamsburg, Kentucky 40769

Contact: Bonnie Buther—Athletics

Phone: (606) 549–8151

<u>Awards</u>

Cheerleading: $250 per semester

Pompon: None

Mascot: $250 per semester

Squads: Varsity

Eligibility: 2.0 GPA   Freshmen eligible? No

MOREHEAD STATE UNIVERSITY

M.S.U., c/o Myron Doan

Room 302, Howell—McDowell

Morehead, Kentucky 40351

Contact: Myron Doan—Student Life

Phone: (606) 783–2014

<u>Awards</u>

Cheerleading: $600 residential fees credit

Pompon: None

Mascot: $600 residential fees credit

Squads: JV, Varsity

Eligibility: 2.0 GPA   Freshmen eligible? Yes

UNIVERSITY OF KENTUCKY

8 Administration Building

Lexington, Kentucky 40506–0032

Contact: Glen Cook—Athletics

Phone: (606) 257–8927

<u>Awards</u>

Cheerleading: In-state tuition

Pompon: None

Mascot: In-state tuition

Squads: Varsity

Eligibility: 3.0 GPA

Freshmen eligible? Only for JV squad

UNIVERSITY OF LOUISVILLE

Sace 102

Louisville, Kentucky 40292

Contact: James Speed—Intermurals

Phone: (502) 588–6707

<u>Awards</u>

Cheerleading: 20–40% tuition

Pompon: None

Mascot: 20–40% tuition

Squads: JV, Varsity

Eligibility: 2.0 GPA   Freshmen eligible? Yes

★LOUISIANA

LOUISIANA STATE UNIVERSITY

P.O. Box 25095

Baton Rouge, Louisiana 70894–5095

Contact: Ashley Kleinptier—Athletics

Phone: (504) 388–1886

<u>Awards</u>

Cheerleading: $1000

Pompon: $640 per semester

Mascot: None

Squads: JV, Varsity

Eligibility: 2.0 GPA   Freshmen eligible? Yes

LOUISIANA TECH UNIVERSITY

P.O. Box 8578 T.S.

Ruston, Louisiana 71272

Contact: Candee Terry—Student Affairs

Phone: (318) 257–3479

<u>Awards</u>

Cheerleading: Living expenses and $400 per
     quarter

Pompon: $300 per year

Mascot: Living expenses and $400 per quarter

Squads: JV, Varsity

Eligibility: 2.0 GPA   Freshmen eligible? Yes

MCNEESE STATE UNIVERSITY
P.O. Box 93260
Lake Charles, Louisiana 70609–3260
Contact: Rochelle Santiago—Athletics
Phone: (318) 475–5068
Awards
Cheerleading: $300–600
Pompon: None
Mascot: None
Squads: Varsity
Eligibility: 2.0 GPA   Freshmen eligible? Yes

NICHOLLS STATE UNIVERSITY
c/o Student Life
P.O. Box 2005
Thibodoux, Louisiana 70310
Contact: Susie Stuchel—Student Life
Phone: (504) 448–4422
Awards
Cheerleading: $100–200 per semester
Pompon: None
Mascot: $100–200 per semester
Squads: Varsity
Eligibility: 2.0 GPA   Freshmen eligible? Yes

NORTHEAST LOUISIANA UNIVERSITY
Brown Annex 112
Monroe, Louisiana 71209–1180
Contact: Jammy Reeder—Student Activities
Phone: (318) 342–5291
Awards
Cheerleading: $375–450
Pompon: $375–450
Mascot: $375–450
Squads: Varsity
Eligibility: 2.0 GPA, full time status
Freshmen eligible? Yes

★MISSISSIPPI

MISSISSIPPI STATE UNIVERSITY
Media Relations Office
P.O. Drawer 5308

Starkville, Mississippi 39762
Contact: Merina Roberson—Athletics
Phone: (601) 325–2450
Awards
Cheerleading: $500 per semester
Pompon: None
Mascot: $500 per semester
Squads: JV, Varsity
Eligibility: 2.5 GPA   Freshmen eligible? Yes

UNIVERSITY OF SOUTHERN MISSISSIPPI
Southern Station Box 10056
Hattiesburg, Mississippi 39406
Contact: Nicole Bartats—Athletics
Phone: (601) 266–4025
Awards
Cheerleading: $200 per semester tuition credit
Pompon: None
Mascot: $200 per semester tuition credit
Squads: Varsity
Eligibility: 2.0 GPA   Freshmen eligible? Yes

★MISSOURI

NORTHWEST MISSOURI STATE UNIVERSITY
1800 University Drive
Maryville, Missouri 64468
Contact: John Yates—Athletics
Phone: (816) 562–1363
Awards
Cheerleading: $1500
Pompon: $200–300 (Captain only)
Mascot: $1500 Boarding
Squads: Varsity
Eligibility: 2.5 GPA   Freshmen eligible? Yes

SOUTHWEST MISSOURI STATE UNIVERISTY
1 University Plaza Missouri
Cape Girardo, Missouri 63701
Contact: Melanie Moore—Univ. Relations
Phone: (314)651–2113
Awards
Cheerleading $300 per year

Pompon: $300 per year
Mascot: None
Squads: JV, Varsity
Eligibility: 2.2 GPA   Freshmen eligible? Yes

★ NEBRASKA

CREIGHTON UNIVERSITY
200 California Plaza
Omaha, Nebraska 78178
Contact: Judy Streitz—Student Activities
Phone: (402) 280–2563
Awards
Cheerleading: $500
Pompon: $500
Mascot: None
Squads: JV, Varsity
Eligibility: 2.0 GPA—JV Cheer; 2.5 GPA—
    Varsity Cheer; 2.5 GPA—Pompon
Freshmen eligible? Yes

★ NEVADA

UNIVERSITY OF NEVADA AT LAS VEGAS
4505 S. Maryland Parkway
Las Vegas, Nevada 89154–0002
Contact: Lori Sims—Cheer
    Sandy Roberts—Dance line
Phone: (702) 895–3846
Awards
Cheerleading: $500 tuition
Pompon: None
Mascot: None
Squads: JV, Varsity
Eligibility: 2.5 GPA, 1 year previous service
Freshmen eligible? Yes

★ NORTH CAROLINA

LENOIR–RHYNE
Box 7227
Hickory, North Carolina 28603
Contact: Laurie Brill—Athletics

Phone: (704) 328–7305
Awards
Cheerleading: $500 per year
Pompon: None
Mascot: None
Squads: JV, Varsity
Eligibility: 2.0 GPA   Freshmen eligible? Yes

★ OHIO

OHIO STATE UNIVERSITY
8193 Linden Leaf Circle
Columbus, Ohio 43235
Contact: Judy Bunting—Athletics
Phone: (614) 847–1232
Awards
Cheerleading: $700 per semester
Pompon: None
Mascot: None
Squads: JV, Varsity
Eligibility: 2.0 GPA   Freshmen eligible? Yes

★ TENNESSEE

MEMPHIS STATE UNIVERSITY
MSU Field House
Room 375
Memphis, Tennessee 38152
Contact: Van VanEaton—Student Affairs
Phone: (901) 678–4730
Awards
Cheerleading: $500
Pompon: $500
Mascot: $500
Squads: JV, Varsity
Eligibility: 2.0 GPA   Freshmen eligible? Yes

★ TEXAS

ANGELO STATE UNIVERSITY
P.O. Box 11016
San Angelo, Texas 76909
Contact: Dirk Hibler—Athletics

Phone: (915) 942–2264
<u>Awards</u>
Cheerleading: $200 per semester (add $100 for every returning year)
Pompon: $100
Mascot: $200 per semester (add $100 for every returning year)
Squads: Varsity
Eligibility: 2.25 GPA   Freshmen eligible? No

SAM HOUSTON STATE UNIVERSITY
P.O. Box 2237
Huntsville, Texas 77341
Contact: Kristi Krier—Student Life
Phone: (409) 294–1726
<u>Awards</u>
Cheerleading: $400 per semester (varsity only)
Pompon: $400 per semester (varsity only)
Mascot: None
Squads: JV, Varsity
Eligibility: 2.0 GPA   Freshmen eligible? Yes

STEPHEN F. AUSTIN STATE UNIVERSITY
1800 North Street
Nacogdoches, Texas 75962
Contact: Dan Wallace—Student Development
Phone: (409) 468–3506
<u>Awards</u>
Cheerleading: $500 per semester
Pompon: $500 per semester
Mascot: $500 per semester
Squads: Varsity
Eligibility: 2.1 GPA   Freshmen eligible? Yes

UNIVERSITY OF TEXAS AT AUSTIN
Texas Cheerleading
Campus Activities Office
Texas Union 4.304
Austin, Texas 78713–7338
Contact: Billy Pope—Athletics

Phone: (512) 471–3065
<u>Awards</u>
Cheerleading: $1000 General, $5000 Minorities
Pompon: $1000 General, $5000 Minorities
Mascot: $1000 General, $5000 Minorities
Squads: Varsity
Eligibility: 2.0 GPA   Freshmen eligible? Yes

WEST TEXAS STATE UNIVERSITY
WT Box 49
Canyon, Texas 79016
Contact: Holly Troth Sponsor—Athletics
Phone: (806) 656–2055
<u>Awards</u>
Cheerleading: $200 per year (Varsity only)
Pompon: None
Mascot: $200 per year
Squads: JV, Varsity
Eligibility: 2.0 GPA   Freshmen eligible? Yes

★VIRGINIA

LIBERTY UNIVERSITY
c/o Athletic Department
1105 Mill Stream Lane
Lynchburg, Virginia 24502
Contact: Tracy Picard—Athletics
Phone: (804) 384–5236
<u>Awards</u>
Cheerleading: $1900–$2900 per year
Pompon: None
Mascot: $800
Squads: JV, Varsity
Eligibility: 2.0 GPA   Freshmen eligible? No

Many spirit organizations also offer scholarships to cheerleaders. Refer to Appendix B to write for more information.

APPENDIX B

SPIRIT ASSOCIATIONS

Contact the following spirit associations for camp or instruction information.

CHEER LTD.
5847 Ramsey Street
Ascot Plaza
Fayetteville, North Carolina 28311
(800) 477–8868

INTERNATIONAL CHEERLEADING FOUNDATION, INC.
10660 Barkley Lane
Shawnee Mission, Kansas 66212

NATIONAL CHEERLEADERS ASSOCIATION
P.O. Box 30674
Dallas, Texas 75230
(214) 213–6364

UNITED SPIRIT ASSOCIATION
2133B Leghorn Street
Mountain View, California 94043
(405) 969–6660

UNIVERSAL CHEERLEADING ASSOCIATION
2535 Horizon Lake Drive, Suite #1
Memphis, Tennessee 38133
(800) 238–0286

APPENDIX C

EATING DISORDER ASSOCIATIONS

The following organizations provide information regarding eating disorders:

AMERICAN ANOREXIA NERVOSA AND BULIMIA
    ASSOCIATION (AABA)
418 East 76th Street
New York, New York 10021
(212) 739–1114

ANOREXIA-BULIMICS ANONYMOUS
P.O. Box 47573
Phoenix, Arizona 85068
(602) 861–3295

ANOREXIA NERVOSA AND RELATED EATING
    DISORDERS, INC. (ANRED)
P.O. Box 5102
Eugene, Oregon 97405
(503) 344–1144

BULIMIA ANOREXIA SELF HELP (BASH)
P.O. Box 39903
St. Louis, Missouri 63139
(314) 567–4080

CENTER FOR THE STUDY OF ANOREXIA AND
    BULIMIA (CSAB)
1 West 91st Street
New York, New York 10024
(212) 595–3449

NATIONAL ANOREXIC AID SOCIETY (NAAS)
1925 East Dublin-Granville Road
Columbus, Ohio 43229
(614) 436–1112

NATIONAL ASSOCIATION OF ANOREXIA NERVOSA
    AND ASSOCIATED DISORDERS (ANAD)
Box 7
Highland Park, Illinois 60035 **Glossary**

GLOSSARY

Anorexia Nervosa: An eating disorder characterized by the fear of fatness; starvation where dramatic weight loss of twenty-five percent of normal body weight is lost within a short amount of time.

Arch: A position in which the back is curved.

Base: The bottom person in the stunt who remains in contact with the floor, supporting the mounter in a stunt.

Bio-electrical Impedance: A method of measuring body fat using precision medical instruments to measure electrical resistance.

Bulimia: An eating disorder characterized by semi-starvation in which bingeing and purging occur.

Calisthenics: A series of exercises used to develop strength, power and balance.

Cardiopulmonary Resuscitation (CPR): A method of rejuvenating a person's heart and breathing functions using artificial breathing and heart massage.

Chant: A short repetitive yell performed continually throughout a game.

Cheer: A longer spirited yell performed only during official breaks of a game.

Compulsive Overeating: An eating disorder characterized by constant consumption of high calorie, high fat food.

Cradle Catch: Occurs when the catcher(s) catch a mounter by holding her around the back and under the thighs.

Dismount: A method used to return to a floor position following a stunt.

Extension: A stunt in which the arms of each base are fully extended above the head, supporting the mounter standing in the palms of the base(s).

Gymnastics Cheer: A cheer involving any use of gymnastics.

Hand Spring: A spring from a standing position to the hands, and back to a standing position.

Heat Stroke: A condition in which the body

reacts to high temperature. Symptoms may include blurred vision, inability to perspire and hypovolemic shock.

Hypothermia: A condition which causes the body temperature to become abnormally low.

Ice Pack: A bag filled with crushed ice, used to reduce swelling.

Jump: A spring into the air with both feet off the ground to a given position with a landing on one or both feet.

Lactic Acid: A product secreted when the muscles are generously exercised; believed to be a cause of muscle soreness.

Layout: A straight or arched position.

Leap: A moving spring position in the air from one foot to the other.

Mounter: The top person in a stunt, who is supported by one or more persons.

Overload: When a muscle or group of muscles are exercised to fatigue.

Partner Stunts: Referred to as double stunts; a maneuver in which at least one mounter is supported by one base.

Pike: A position in which the body is bent at the hips and legs are straight out in a ninety degree angle.

Pirouette: A turn in standing position on one leg to a different direction.

Pom Pon Routine: A dance routine performed with pom pons.

Primary Foods: The basic four food groups: breads and cereals, fruits and vegetables, meats and proteins, and milk and dairy products.

Pyramid: A stunt involving one or more mounters who are supported by one or more bases and linked together.

Routine: A choreographed combination of dance steps.

Skinfold Calipers: An instrument used to "clinch" the skin and measure body fat.

Split: A movement or sitting position in which the legs are spread apart in alignment or sideways one in front of the other.

Spotter: A person in continual contact with the stunt, providing assistance as needed.

Straddle: A position where the legs are straight out and apart.

Stag: A leap or pose in which one leg is bent and the other is straight.

Strength: The power of muscles to resist force.

Toxic Shock Syndrome (TSS): A condition primarily associated with women using tampons while menstruating. Symptoms include vomiting, high fever, and disorientation; the condition is often fatal.

Traditional Cheerleading: Organized group yell leading characterized by the use of motions and stunt performance.

Tuck: A position in which the body is bent at the hips and the knees are held tightly up to the chest.

Underwater Weighing: A method of determining body fat percentage involving the measurement of weight and water displacement while submerged in a tub of water.

INDEX

PHOTO AND ILLUSTRATION CREDITS